Bliss

The Smart Girl's Guide to Friends

Lisa Smosarski

Piccadilly Press • London

*To my oldest friends, Zoë, Tony and Tam –
and my newest friend, Lydia.*

First published in Great Britain in 2001
by Piccadilly Press Ltd.,
5 Castle Road, London NW1 8PR

Text copyright © Emap Elan, 2001
Cover photograph © Telegraph Colour Library, 2001

All rights reserved. No part of this publication may be
reproduced, stored in a retrieval system, or transmitted
in any form or by any means electronic, mechanical,
photocopying, recording or otherwise, without the
prior permission of the copyright owner.

The right of Emap Elan to be identified as Author of this
work has been asserted by them in accordance with the
Copyright, Designs and Patents Act, 1988.

Photoypeset from the author's disc
in 10.5 Futura Book

A catalogue record for this book
is available from the British Library

ISBN: 1 85340 674 0 (paperback)

1 3 5 7 9 10 8 6 4 2

Printed and bound in Great Britain
by Bookmarque Ltd

Design by Louise Millar

Lisa Smosarski is the Features Director of Bliss *magazine.
She lives in West Hampstead, London.
This is her first book.*

CONTENTS

SECTION 1 – MATES ARE GREAT
Chapter 1 Why Do We Need Friends?   5
Chapter 2 What Makes a Good Friend?   11
Chapter 3 Making Friends   18
Chapter 4 Friendship Types   30
Chapter 5 Best Friends   46
Chapter 6 Maintaining Your Friendships   53
Chapter 7 Are You a Good Friend?   61

SECTION 2 – FRIENDSHIP DILEMMAS
Chapter 8 Your Friendship Problems   79
Chapter 9 When You Make Mistakes   89
Chapter 10 When Friendship Turns Sour   99
Chapter 11 Three's a Crowd   114
Chapter 12 The Green-Eyed Monster   122
Chapter 13 Compatibility   127
Chapter 14 Just Good Friends   134
Chapter 15 Growing Apart   141
Chapter 16 Bullying   147
APPENDIX   154
INDEX   156

SECTION 1
MATES ARE GREAT

"Friends are like stars. Even when you can't see them, you know they're always there for you."
Text message from Mel B to Emma Bunton

Chapter 1

WHY DO WE NEED FRIENDS?

You're probably thinking that's the daftest question in the world. It's obvious why we need friends . . . isn't it? After all, there are loads of reasons, like:

- Friends make us laugh.
- Friends know when we're sad and make us feel better.

- You can tell your friends stuff you wouldn't tell anyone else.
- It's cool to just have a companion, someone to hang out with.
- Friends can give you advice.
- Friends are fun!

Without even knowing it, your friends are probably one of the most important parts of your life. They can offer you the help and support nobody else can because they know you inside out. Can you imagine telling your mum Jason Roberts tried to grab your boob when you were snogging? She'd hit the roof, right? She doesn't even know you've snogged anyone, let alone who Jason Roberts is! But tell your mate and she'll give you the answer you're looking for – "He did what? He's so cheeky. I'll sort him out! Hope you told him where to go . . ." In fact, she can think of a hundred right things to say.

A FRIEND IN NEED

How many times have you heard oldies mumble, "Well, dear, a friend in need really is a friend indeed." Probably about a thousand, right? The thing is, there is actually some truth in that. Think about it. When do you really know who your friends are? When you've got a problem.

Rachel, 15, from Nottingham, discovered who her friends were when her parents got divorced. *"It was possibly the worst time of my life,"* Rachel admits. *"I really felt like my life was falling apart. My mum and dad were so involved with their own problems, they didn't realise I was totally devastated. My friends were my lifeline. So, after opening my heart to my friends, I was completely crushed to find out it was round the whole school the next day. Only three of my friends really stood by me, which is how I got to know they were real friends.*

"The whole experience made us all much closer, which is why we all now know we can always rely on each other – through thick and thin. It sounds weird, but those girls blabbing my personal business around the school was the best thing that could have ever happened because I got to find out who I could really trust."

Your true friends really do stand out when

you've got a problem, which is why it's equally important to do the same for your mates when they need your help. Friends can help you survive the toughest times in your life, which is why we all need to have them.

FRIENDS OVER FAMILY

There's a big difference between friends and family. OK, so whatever happens your family will always be family (blood is thicker than water, and all that), but your friends are the people who really know you. Your mum and dad love you to bits, and will always try to help you out. They're tops when it comes to advice on school, making sure you're OK, and generally being there for you. But sometimes they'll find it hard to discuss matters that are important to you – or perhaps they may struggle to understand things that are fundamental in your life. The average mum and dad may find it hard to talk about boys with you – after all, in their eyes, you're their precious perfect princess who's not into snogging at all! Sometimes they seem to think you're happiest sitting in front of 'Sesame Street' playing with Barbie!

Which is why it's great when friends step in. They're experiencing the same things as you, and feeling the same emotions, so they can understand exactly what you mean when you talk about your friends, boys, clothes and make-up. (Come on, when did you last enjoy a family outing to New Look?)

Friends can also reassure you in a different way to your mum or teachers. It's always nice to hear oldies tell you you're normal, or that we all experience the same things. But where's the evidence? You need a friend for that.

"I always used to worry I was weird, a freak of nature, because I hadn't snogged anyone yet," says 16-year-old Jane, from Scunthorpe. *"Everyone at school seemed to have copped off with at least 10 boys. I worried about it for ages. When I was at school I could hear the other girls talking about getting off with lads at parties – I just assumed everyone was doing it. I told my mum but she just laughed and told me I shouldn't be worrying about stupid things like that. So I talked to my best mates Sammy and Lucy. It turned out Sammy had only snogged one boy (and it had*

been a disaster anyway) and Lucy still hadn't snogged anyone – although she had lied to another friend that she had. We soon realised that probably only a few of the girls we knew had had a lot of action, and the rest were just lying to fit in. Without talking to my mates I never would have known that."

NORA NO MATES

So imagine a life without friends. Not only would you have no one to turn to for advice and support, but you'd also miss out on girly nights in, drooling over Craig David, stuffing your face with pizza and choccies, and giving each other makeovers.

Friends make you feel absolutely fantastic about yourself, and give you the biggest laugh of your life. Because you tend to make friends with people with similar interests and senses of humour, no one will make you crack up more than your buddies.

Try to remember how sad it is to feel alone, and if you do spot someone sitting on their own, why not go and say hello? You may just make their day – and a great new friend as well.

Chapter 2

WHAT MAKES A GOOD FRIEND?

There are all sorts of things that make a good friend. Think about your friends and the reasons you like them. It may be because they're funny, silly, sensible or caring – or it may be that you both love 'EastEnders'. Whatever it is, there can be lots of reasons why you really love your mates.

UNDERSTANDING

"I really love my friend Jo because I know she understands me like nobody else does. She knows when I'm happy, sad, nervous, or just feeling stupid! It's like she lives inside my head – which is totally cool." Natalie, 16, Sutton Coldfield

Understanding is a really important part of a good friendship. You know you've found a great mate when they understand you like no one else can. Often your friendship will develop because you've grown up together and you've had the same life experience. That means you can really understand what your friend has been through and what she's going through now – because you've been through exactly the same experiences.

Spending time with a friend will also help you develop your understanding of each other. After you've hung out with a friend for a while you'll find out if she prefers chocolate or crisps, 'Neighbours' or 'Coronation Street', maths or English. And then you'll discover how she handles herself in certain situations. Does she cry at films? Will she argue if someone's horrible to her, or will she just walk away? Will she snog on a first date? Is she sensitive or tough? Only by spending time with someone will you answer these questions (and a whole load more), and eventually you'll start to know the answer before you've even asked the question.

But the best bit about understanding in a friendship is that it's great for everyone – knowing someone understands you really well is lovely, and it's also pretty cool to know someone else inside out, too.

TRUST

"I know I've found a good friend when I realise I can trust them – even with my deepest, darkest, secrets. I think I've found very few people who I could trust with anything, which is why I know they will always be a good friend to me."
Shelley, 17, London

Trust is an essential part of a good friendship – it's kind of like strawberries and cream, fish and chips and Posh and Becks; you just can't have one without the other.

Think about it, if a 'friend' breaks your trust by blabbing a secret or bitching about you behind your back then you know they're a bad friend. After all, it's no fun being mates with someone who may let you down, or even turn on you, at any time. It takes time to earn trust with a friend – after all, you're not going to go running up to someone you've just met and tell them about the time you sneezed in the face of the fittest lad in school.

You'd just be asking for trouble.

Once you've got to know a new friend well you'll have a better idea if you can trust her. A good judge of this is to listen to how she talks about other friends. Does she blab their secrets or tell you stuff you shouldn't really know? If so, you should tread carefully – you don't want to be the subject of gossip for her and her other mates. But, if you think she's telling you stuff in confidence then you've probably found a friend you can trust – after all, she's taking a risk too.

> **Friendship Tip:** In order to be a great mate it's important to remember that you have to be as trustworthy as you are trusting. In other words, if a friend tells you a secret make sure it stays that way.

FUN

"I love my mates so much because they're the funniest people I know. We spend the whole time cracking up, and have got hundreds of in-jokes. Some people at school think we're a bit sad because we're always giggling, but I don't care. My mates are well funny." Zoe, 15, Stratford

It's weird what makes people laugh. Some people crack up when their mates fall over, others get the best laugh from joke-telling, and – weirder still – some people chuckle out loud to things like Shakespeare plays. Everyone finds something funny, which is why it's so good when you meet a person who laughs at the same things as you do, or who's just the funniest person you've ever met.

RELIABILITY

"I think the best thing about my friends is that, whatever happens, they'll always be there for me. Even if I called them up in the middle of the night to talk about something that was bugging me I know they'd be prepared to help me out. It sounds really boring, but they're great friends because they're 100% reliable." Cara, 16, Weston-Super-Mare

It's very important to have friends you can rely on. It would be really upsetting to turn to a friend with a problem only for her to tell you she was too busy to listen. Or for you to arrange a top night out and then have her cancel at the last minute so she can go out with her new boyfriend instead. Obviously, you can't expect your friends to drop everything every time you have a minor crisis, or just to come running because you're bored. But if you value your friendship it's essential to make the effort to be a person your friends can rely on.

FORGIVENESS

"Sometimes me and my best friend have big arguments. We stand in each other's faces and literally scream for five minutes. Then we'll both sit down, take a deep breath, and within minutes we'll be laughing about it. Neither of us ever holds a grudge – about anything." Lucy, 17, Bath

However great mates you are with someone, it's inevitable that you will have some sort of run-in. Like Lucy you may have a big screaming match, or you may just get annoyed about something your mate has said or done. The important thing is to recognise that this is just a part of being human. It's almost impossible to hang out with someone regularly and not get frustrated by the odd little thing, but as long as you're prepared to forgive and forget you'll be back to normal again in no time. Think about how you handle arguments with your mum and dad, or with brothers and sisters. Eventually you always forgive them because deep down you know they love you loads. Well, there's no difference with your mates. We all say stuff we regret in arguments, which is why it's important to be prepared to forgive and forget if you do fall out with your mates.

Unless it's really serious, don't be stubborn or difficult, you can just shrug it off and give your friend a big hug – within minutes you'll have forgotten what you were even rowing about. Or, even better, talk through the problem and learn from your mistakes. Your friendship will be even stronger for it.

Chapter 3

MAKING FRIENDS

OK, so we've established why friends are so great, and we know the qualities we look for in our mates, but how do you go about making new friends? It's not like there are any set rules, so it's almost impossible to 'learn' how to do it. But there a few tips you can follow to make the process of meeting new people a whole lot easier.

The problem:
Where do I go to meet new friends?
The solution:
This is an easy one to solve. You don't need an official place – like a meeting new mates club –

in order to find potential friends. Take a look around you. Everywhere you look you can see girls like you who would probably like to be your mate, but if you're still not sure here are a few suggestions . . .

SCHOOL

Obviously your school is the best – and easiest – place to make new friends. If you've just moved to a new school you may feel uncomfortable because everyone you meet seems to have enough friends already. But, let's face it, you can never have too many buddies. So take advantage of the fact that throughout the day there are loads of chances for you to meet new people.

IN LESSONS

When you go into a classroom don't immediately head to an empty desk. If you spot an empty seat next to someone go and ask if it's free. Then, throughout the lesson, you've got a chance to introduce yourself to your desk friend. And you won't be stuck for small talk either because there will be loads going on in the classroom that you can talk about. And remember, asking questions is a great way to open a conversation because you don't have to do all the talking.

Why not try asking questions like these?

- So, what's the teacher really like?
- Do you know where we've got to in the textbook?
- Do you get loads of homework?

You never know, you may be asked to pair off to do some work, which means you'll be chatting without even thinking about it.

AT BREAK-TIME

Break-time is probably the worst time of the day when you don't know anyone at school. Hopefully somebody will come up and say "hi". But if they don't it's up to you to take a big breath and be really mature. Try to spot someone you've been in a class with and wander over and say hello. You can say anything you want, but if you're really stuck for words why not try something like: "Hiya, my name's Lisa and I've just started here. I spotted you in form class today and was just wondering if you could tell me what this school's really like . . .

I mean, are the teachers complete witches?"

Then get back into the habit of asking questions. The key is to tap into the one thing you have in common, and that one thing (to begin with at least) is school. And remember don't give up if someone gives you the brush-off. Just smile and say, "No worries, I can see you're busy," before moving on to someone who looks a little friendlier. The truth is some people are shy and others are plain unfriendly, but most people will be more than happy to have a chat (and check out the new kid)! So don't be scared about making the first move.

If, on the other hand, you've already got mates at the school, but you just want a few more, then follow the same advice. Making new friends is all about talking to people, so don't be scared to make the first move. And if you do spot a new girl, why not approach her first? (Trust me, it's much less scary for you than it is for her!) Invite her to hang out with you and your friends, and then start asking questions about her life – where was she before? What's she into? etc. . . .

CLUBS, SPORT AND HOBBIES

Clubs where you do a sport or hobby are fantastic places to meet new people because you'll be surrounded by others with the same interests as you – in other words, perfect friendship material. So use that as the starting place for your first conversation. Then, the next time you meet up make sure you say hello and have a little chat – it won't be long before you've swapped numbers and are chatting all the time, or meeting outside the club.

FRIENDS OF FRIENDS

There are probably potential new friends already in your life. Lots of your existing mates will have friends or relatives that you don't know. So why not throw a party and get everyone to invite all of their friends, not just your usual crowd? If it all goes according to plan you'll all be making some great new mates.

Still not sure what to do? Here are some of the most common problems – and solutions:

The problem:
I don't know what to say when I actually do meet new people.

The solution:
There's no right or wrong when it comes to talking to new people. Some of you will find it just comes naturally – you've mastered the art of chitchat. However, others of you will get completely stuck for words. But don't worry if that's you – here a few simple pointers to get you chatting at ease.

- Never try to be someone you're not. By that, I mean don't go waltzing over to a potential friend and start banging on about Marilyn Manson when you're actually a hardcore S Club fan. Not only will you get pretty stuck for words should the person you're talking to be a complete Manson-ite, but you'll become friends with someone for all the wrong reasons. You want your friends to like you for you – not the person you think you should be.
- Usually you will know at least one thing about the person you want to be friends with – use

this as your conversation starter. So if you know this girl is in the drama club, use this for your opening line. Ask a question and she'll find it easier to chat too. And, if she's keen to make new mates as well, then she'll probably ask you some stuff in return.

- Let's imagine you don't know this girl from Eve. If that really is the case then you're going to have to start from scratch. Introduce yourself and tell her one thing about yourself (eg: "My name's Lisa. I go to Friern Barnet County School."). Now throw the same question open to her – "So what about you? Do you go to school around here?" You'll get a short reply, so you'll still need to put some work in. Why not tell her why you're talking to her? Let's imagine you're both at a new dance class and don't know anyone else. So you may say: "Do you know anyone else in this class?" or "Have you been here before?" Then you can add, "I feel a bit like the new kid because I don't know anyone here." Your new friend will be able to tell you about her own experiences, have a good understanding of why you're chatting, and also be able to ask you any questions she has on her mind. Whatever happens, you'll soon be chatting. If you do run up against a monosyllabic, yes–no brick wall, then rethink your strategy. She's probably just shy (not moody) so try asking questions she will have to answer more fully, like, "What do you think about . . . ?", "What's the best/worst thing about . . . ?" She'll have no choice but to chat!

> **Friendship Tip:** Remember – questions, questions, questions. The best way to get someone chatting is to ask them about their own life. After all, that's the one thing we all know inside out and can talk about for as long as we need to.

The problem:
I'm just too shy – I can't do any of these things.
The solution:
If you really are too shy to do any of these things, then you have to rethink your strategy. Follow the flowchart overleaf to find the solution to your problem.

THE SMART GIRL'S GUIDE TO **FRIENDS**

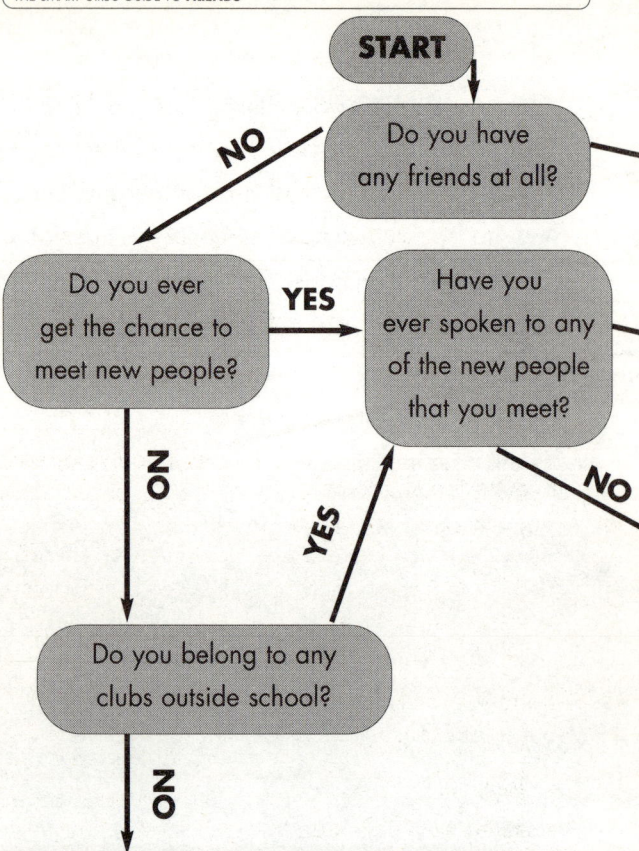

START

Do you have any friends at all?

NO →

Do you ever get the chance to meet new people?

YES → Have you ever spoken to any of the new people that you meet?

NO ↓

Do you belong to any clubs outside school?

YES ↑ (back to "Have you ever spoken to any of the new people that you meet?")

NO ↓

Tell your mum and dad you're having trouble making new friends because you're too shy (don't be embarrassed, they'll really want to help you). Then ask them if they can enroll you in a club outside school so you have a chance to meet some new people.

26

MAKING FRIENDS

YES

Ask your friends to introduce you to some new people. Tell them you're just too shy to do it yourself. Once you've been introduced try to start a conversation. It may take some time but you'll get there in the end.

YES

If you're too shy to go up to someone and start talking then you need to take a different route. Try using non-verbal communication (NVC) to introduce yourself, or at least to make yourself more familiar. NVC is stuff like smiling in recognition whenever you see someone, or physically moving towards a person you'd like to talk to – that way they know you're open to having a chat if they fancy it.

If you've already spoken to some of these new people, it's important to keep up the familiarity next time you see them. You don't have to jump on them like an old mate every time you meet up, but it's really useful to smile, say hello, and ask how they are. Sometimes this may be it – other times you'll talk more. You'll soon suss it out.

THE TIMELINE OF A NEW FRIENDSHIP

Not all friendships are the same. Sometimes you may meet a person you think is nice, but you may not have much in common with them. Or maybe they're just different to you. These people are great to chat to occasionally, but you probably won't do much more. However, when you do meet someone you really click with the friendship will probably develop along the following lines . . .

Step one

It's meet and greet time. You're using this time to introduce yourselves and find out a little about each other. It will be made up of questions, politeness, and general niceties!

Step two

This is the time when you're really starting to click. Instead of just chatting about your general lives, you'll start to understand each other. Chatting becomes easier and you'll soon be talking about all sorts of stuff – like what was on telly last night, or about a boy you fancy. You'll begin to trust this person more and more.

Step three
By now you'll know each other fairly well, and will probably be prepared to take your friendship a step further. You'll probably swap phone numbers or emails and start keeping in touch, or you may arrange to meet up to go shopping, or just to hang out.

Step four
Your friendship is really in full swing now and you'll be having a good laugh together. But this is also the time for sharing – you'll start to disclose little secrets about yourselves, and will probably start offering and asking for advice. It's a test in trust and understanding – a real make or break time.

Step five
Now you know each other inside out you'll know you have a real friendship that will last. This isn't a new friend any more, this is a great friend!

Chapter 4

FRIENDSHIP TYPES

We all have different types of friends. It's kind of like outfits – we have one to suit every occasion. We have friends that make us laugh and friends who are there for us when we cry. We have mates to do different things with (one of your friends might love rollerblading with you, but the rest may rather have red hot pokers stuck in their eyes), friends for different moods (there are just some mates who are more goofy and daft than others) and we have friends for different situations in life – like at school, work, or when we're out partying.

Everyone's different, which kind of explains

why our friends are all so, well, different too. But however kooky and individual we all are, there are a few friendship types we're all likely to encounter:

THE FAIR-WEATHER FRIEND

We all have a fair-weather friend. She's the one who sticks to your side like glue when the going's good. But as soon as there's a sniff of trouble in the air she'll break the sound barrier trying to get out of your life as fast as humanly possible. She only wants to be around happy people, so if you've got a problem don't go crying to her.

THE HOT-COLD FRIEND

Hot-cold friend is a relative of the fair-weather friend. She's your best mate when you first meet. In fact, she can't see you enough or do enough for you. But as soon as she meets a new girl to hang out with you're yesterday's news and she's off chasing her about instead. Her poor new mate will suffer the same fate, too. The trouble is, this girl just chases the highs associated with meeting and getting to know a new friend.

Mind you, that will all change if something

exciting happens to you. If you decide to have a party, land yourself the lead role in the school show, or win a competition, you'll soon find her back at your side attempting to lap up your glory. Charming. But she'll be off once more as quick as you can say "my life's really normal again". Don't take it personally, though – she's the one missing out on a real friendship because she's so busy trying to meet the next most exciting and popular girl in town.

THE ACQUAINTANCE

The more places you go in life, the more people you'll get to know. You won't necessarily build up fantastic friendships with all of these people, even if you do really like them. But whenever you do bump into one another you'll make the effort to catch up and have a really nice chat. You know that'll be it until the next time your paths cross, but you're both happy with that, which is what makes this friendship so lovely. It's easy and it's nice.

THE SCHOOL FRIEND

Think about all the people you know at school. Some people you probably don't really talk to, some you hang out with all the time, and others you just talk to when you're at school. These are your school-only friends. You'll have a good laugh with them while you're at school, you may sit next to them in lessons and spend break-times catching up on gossip. But whenever you're out of school you don't really keep in touch. You're friends with these people because you go to school with them – that's your common ground, and you're going to enjoy it while it lasts.

THE BOY MATE

This is a bit of a funny one. Loads of people will argue (until their heads explode) that it's impossible to have a purely platonic relationship between a girl and a boy. But that's not always true.

"My best friend is a boy called Tony," says 16-year-old Anne from London. *"We got to know each other when I worked with him on Saturdays in his dad's shop. We'd always have a top laugh together, but that was all it was. There was never*

going to be any romance – we just didn't fancy each other. Whenever we met up we'd talk about the boys I fancied, and he'd try to tell me how to get my hands on my crushes. He even set me up on a few dates with his mates. And he always knew what to say if I'd had a big row with a boyfriend. We just understood each other like nobody else could – he's the only person who knows absolutely everything about me.

"The weirdest thing is how other people react. We've lost count of the amount of times we've been called boyfriend and girlfriend. And we're bored of arguing with our other friends who come out with stuff like: 'Oh, friends, really. Come on, what are you two up to?' It's just so dull! Our friendship is 100% platonic – and I'm really top mates with his girlfriend, too."

OK, so not all boys will have innocent motives like Tony, but there are lots of guys out there who you'll get on with, and who you'll just want to be buddies with.

THE BOY MAGNET

This is the one friend who'll make you want to scream "What about me?" at the top of your voice. Without even trying, everywhere this girl goes boys literally drop at her feet. They think she's stunning, funny, and ideal girlfriend material. Whenever you meet new boys they'll call you over. "This time," you think, "I've pulled." But all they really want to do is find out if she's single. Life is so unfair! So it's probably a good idea to keep her well away from your crush until you've got him completely hooked because, without meaning it, she'll swan in and steal his attention.

THE KOOKY KID

This is one of the best friends any girl can have because she's totally bonkers! She lives on another planet, and will always keep you entertained with her kooky ways and mad ideas. You don't often ask her for advice because her ideas are too off-the-wall, but whenever you want to cheer yourself up she's definitely the best girl to turn to. She doesn't necessarily realise she's a complete eccentric, but she's totally loving and caring and will never say a bad word about anyone. However, she does have the potential to be a bit blunt – but don't feel bad if she's, er, direct with you; her honesty is a great attribute and means you'll always know where you stand with her.

THE CONTROL FREAK

The control freak, as her name suggests, loves to take control of everything. At times this'll be great because you can sit back and let her do all the work – and she'll thank you for it. Fancy a night out with the girls? She'll arrange it. Need to return a pair of shoes? She'll do it for you. But her bossiness does wear a bit thin when she starts telling you what to do. Unfortunately this is the one thing the control freak can't control – her own bossiness. If you find her trying to control you too much you have to tell her straight – she'll appreciate your strength of character. You don't want to lose her as a mate, but you don't want her to take over your life either.

THE LEECH

Uh-oh, she's a bit of a baddy in your life. The leech sticks to your side like glue. Unfortunately she doesn't have enough tact to realise that sometimes you'll want to do things without her. Her constant need for attention, obsession with hanging out with you and general wishy-washyness will slowly drain the life out of you. So tell her to tone it down before you say something you really regret.

THE PARTY PAL

This girl is a brilliant laugh. You absolutely adore hanging out with her. When you plan a night out you know it's going to be huge – a real night to remember. She loves to party and will have you flailing your limbs across the dance floor before you can yell "disco diva". At the same time, however, you've never spent much time really getting to know one another. You don't know much about each other's lives which means you're far from best buddies, but if you ever fancy letting your hair down and forgetting all your worries then this is the friend to call.

THE LONG-TERMER

This is the friend you've had since your nappy-wearing days. You've been through everything together and have a very special friendship. You know all there is to know about each other. And you know that if you've come this far together you'll always be "forever friends". She's the one person you can always be yourself with, and can share all your serious times with. You both have other friends, and sometimes you find it hard to meet up as a crowd because you're all quite different. But this is the one friend you'll always make time to meet up with one on one.

Want to find out more? Now find out what type of friends you've got.

WHO'S WHO?

Think carefully about one of your friends. Now concentrate on the following questions and ring the answer that you think would most accurately describe your friend's reaction to each of the scenarios.

FRIENDSHIP TYPES

1 You've had a really bad day and are in floods of tears. What does your friend do?

a Hug you until you've calmed down, listen to what you've got to say, then tell you exactly what you've been longing to hear.

b Give you a hug and remind you of all the other times this has happened. You feel better when you realise you got over all those other times, too. Your life isn't a total disaster!

c Give you a hug, sing you a little song, and start telling you jokes in funny voices until you can't help laughing.

d Invite you over to her house for a makeover – a bit of pampering will make you feel much better.

e Give you a quick hug then tell you to stop feeling sorry for yourself and to pull yourself together.

f Pat you on the back and leave you on your own for "alone time", before hurrying off to meet her other mates.

g Look surprised – and then give you a big hug until you feel better.

h Take you under her wing and smother you with so much attention you feel like locking her in a cupboard.

i Take you clubbing. It's the only way to solve the blues.

j Nothing. She's nowhere to be seen.

2 You fancy a big night out. You really want to throw a massive party. But what does your friend suggest?

a She tells you not to worry – she'll organise a party. You don't have to do anything (except have fun)!

b A reunion with all your old mates you haven't seen for ages.

c She reckons you should have a party, too. She offers to help with the arrangements.

d A night out on the pull – she knows about a party a boy in the sixth form is throwing and thinks your luck will be in.

e It's up to you – just let her know when it's all organised.

f She thinks a party sounds like a great idea – can she bring some of her friends?

g She thinks you should have a fancy dress party, and all go dressed as your teachers. Well, it could be fun.

h A party? That's the best idea she's ever heard! This is going to be the biggest party ever thrown.

i She agrees – you always make such great decisions.

j A party sounds great – she'll see you there if everyone else is going.

3 Your friend invites you over for dinner. What does she cook for you?

a She doesn't know what you like, so she does a buffet with loads of bits to choose from.

b Your all-time favourite dinner.

c She wants to treat you, so she buys in your fave takeaway instead.

d A big chocolate fondue.

e Her favourite dinner.

f Fish-fingers, chips and beans – well, it's simple, isn't it?

g She's invited a couple of lads over to make it a double date, and ends up cooking her date's favourite dinner. In typical boy style, it's burgers and chips.

h Something ridiculously extravagant. Well, only the best will do.

i She doesn't bother. When you get there she's changed her mind and decided you both need a night out clubbing instead.

j She asks you to decide. She really doesn't want to mess this up for you.

4 You're practising for your English oral. Your teacher asks everyone to stand up and say something about their friend. Your friend stands up and says of you:

a She's a really big flirt – boys fall over themselves to be near her.

b She's caring, loving and a fantastic friend. I don't know what I'd do without her.

c She can be a bit indecisive and needs someone to look after her.

d She's got some really dodgy habits (nose picking, smelly feet, burps a lot). That's what I like best about her.

e She's not changed since she was little – she's still great.
f She always makes the effort to be nice to people she doesn't know.
g She's really popular – I love that.
h She always seems so happy.
i She's the most wonderful girl in the world. I'd love to be just like her.
j She's a party animal.

5 Which of these descriptions best sums up your friend?

a Understanding, trusting, fun.
b Polite, pleasant, chatty.
c Committed, loyal, reliable.
d Indecisive, unreliable, excitable.
e Crazy, individual, outgoing.
f Bossy, organised, strong.
g Flirty, affectionate, attractive.
h Outgoing, energetic, crazy.
i Fussy, fickle, attentive.
j Clingy, determined, exhausting.

Now add up your scores and discover your friend's character type.

1 a 10 b 9 c 7 d 6 e 4 f 2 g 1 h 5 i 8 j 3
2 a 4 b 9 c 10 d 6 e 2 f 1 g 7 h 8 i 5 j 3
3 a 1 b 9 c 10 d 7 e 4 f 2 g 6 h 3 i 8 j 5
4 a 6 b 10 c 4 d 7 e 9 f 1 g 2 h 3 i 5 j 8
5 a 10 b 1 c 9 d 2 e 7 f 4 g 6 h 8 i 3 j 5

50
She's your . . . best friend.

45–49
She's your . . . long-term friend.

40–44
She's your . . . party pal.

35–39
She's your . . . kooky friend.

30–34
She's your . . . boy-magnet friend.

25–29
She's your . . . leech friend.

20–24
She's your . . . control freak friend.

14–19
She's your . . . hot–cold friend.

8–13
She's your . . . fair-weather friend.

7 and less
She's your . . . acquaintance.

Now take another look at the friendship descriptions in this chapter, and find out what your mate is like.

Chapter 5

BEST FRIENDS

"I have one best friend who I share absolutely everything with. She's like a sister to me. We're never apart – we do everything together. I think we'd be lost without each other."
Judy, 14, Liverpool

"I have a group of friends and we are all 'best mates'. It would be impossible and unfair to name one of those as being more important than the others are – I just couldn't have one best buddy. But I guess that means I'm lucky."
Manjit, 15, Swansea

"I have one friend who I've grown up with called Michelle: we've always done everything together and we call each other 'best friends'. Recently we've been doing a lot of things apart from one another, but I still call her my best friend because I know she would be there for me if I needed her."
Camilla, 16, Brighton

Everyone has a different idea of what a best friend is, and what having – or being – a best friend means. Some of us think having a best friend is a bit like having a sister. Some of us think you can only have one best friend – that there's only one person you can share a really special bond with. Others think you can have lots of different best pals. And then there's another group of people who think you just have "friends", and none of them are better than the others.

WHAT IS A BEST FRIEND?

There's no right answer to this. After all, we already understand that everyone has a different idea of who and what this person is. But there are a few qualities which best friends usually have.

Think of the person you consider to be your best friend. Then look at the list below. Tick off all the attributes you think apply to your buddy.

1. We tell each other everything. ❑
2. She knows me better than anyone else. ❑
3. We like doing the same stuff. ❑
4. She understands me really well. ❑
5. I would trust her with anything. ❑
6. She's always there for me. ❑
7. We laugh at the same things. ❑
8. She's the first person I always turn to – good or bad. ❑
9. She gets excited if I do well at something (and vice versa). ❑
10. I want to hang out with her all the time. ❑

If you ticked six or more of those boxes it's probably safe to say you're best buddies – but remember, you may be lucky and have more than one.

Why do we need best friends?

It's important for us all to feel we've got friends who know us well and who we can trust, which is why we need best friends. Best friends give us advice, listen to our problems, hang out with us, keep us company, help us out on shopping trips and have a laugh with us – and we can do the same for them.

AVOIDING THE PITFALLS

Having a best friend can be a bit like having a boyfriend or a brother and sister – although you're really close there can be certain things that put a downer on your relationship. These can be avoided, but you've got to watch out for the warning signs.

OVERKILL

The problem:

You see each other every night, talk on the phone twice a day, and generally spend all your time together. But now you're getting annoyed with each other – and are even running out of things to talk about.

The solution:

Stop spending all your time together. It's really hard to spend that much time with anyone – after all, we all need our own space. Start spending a few nights apart and find something new to do, or find some new people to hang out with. Then, when you do meet your best bud, you'll have missed each other loads and will have far more news to catch up on.

POSSESSIVENESS/JEALOUSY
The problem:
You're so used to spending all your time together that if your friend does do something different you find yourself getting jealous and even arguing about it. You're in a horrible situation where neither of you can be friendly with anyone else without the other being well annoyed.

The solution:
This is a really unhealthy situation to find yourself in, and it will finish off your friendship in next to no time. You're too dependent on your friend, and that can be suffocating. So find some new interests and be nicer when she tells you she's doing something else. After all, you don't need to be jealous. It's not that she doesn't value your friendship, but we all need the space to do our own thing.

COMPETITIVENESS
The problem:
Throughout your childhood you two have been mates – and everything's been fine. But now a competitive streak is emerging. You both want to be first to start your periods, snog a boy, and go out clubbing. Or you compete to be best at sport, schoolwork, or even in popularity. Instead of working as a team you've started to turn on each other.

The solution:
This is a problem you need to talk to each other about – otherwise you'll start to really resent one another. Friends should be pleased for each other when they do something well, not jealous. Tell your friend about your jealousy, and no doubt she'll admit hers too. Then sit down and work out how you can achieve things together, that way you get double the pleasure because you get to share the glory.

Friendship Tip: All friends go through ups and downs – it's all part of being a grown-up (yawn). But if you do see a problem emerging make the effort to sit down and talk it through – it's never as bad as it seems, and you'll be best buds again in no time.

Chapter 6

MAINTAINING YOUR FRIENDSHIPS

Once you've found some good mates and settled down into a comfortable friendship, you've still got to work to make it last. You can't just sit back and expect your friendship to be great. Like all relationships, you have to put some effort in. It's also important to ensure that both of you put an equal amount of effort in – it wouldn't be fair for just one of you to always be working harder than the other. But the good thing is, putting effort into a friendship isn't as tough as it sounds – all it takes is a little bit of give and take.

THE RIGHTS AND WRONGS OF FRIENDSHIPS

KEEPING IN TOUCH

Wrong:
"I always wait for my friend to call me. She seems to be really busy all the time, so it's easier for her to find the time." Maria, 14, Enfield

This is an example of expecting your friend to do all the work. Maria doesn't make the effort to call her friend. In the past her friend has made the effort to contact her – but this won't last for ever. Maria's friend will soon get tired of making all the effort, to a point where she may stop calling altogether. If this is the case what will Maria do? It'll be up to her to put the effort in, but by then the friendship may already be over.

Right:
"Me and my best friend seem to take it in turns to call each other. It's really not deliberate (we're not that sad), but it just happens like that. I guess we

both think it's important to keep in touch."
Carrie, 15, Warrington

Carrie and her friend have a really balanced and fair relationship. They both put an equal amount of effort in, and really reap the benefits of having a good friendship. There may be times when one makes more calls, or puts more effort in, but they both understand that in order for the friendship to work long-term they need to treat each other equally.

ADVICE

Wrong:
"I always seem to be giving my friend advice. Every day she has a personal crisis. I'd never turn her away, but there never seems to be time to talk about my life or about what I'm going through. It's always about her." Kelly, 16, Croydon

This is a really unfair situation. Kelly is being a great friend – she always listens, always doles out advice, and is never unavailable for her mate. But by doing this and not returning the favour, her friend has begun to treat her like a doormat. Kelly doesn't have the same support from her friend. She needs to tell her friend how she feels or equal the balance by reducing her availability for her friend's minor nightmares.

Right:

"Most of the time my friend and I spend our time having a laugh. But I am always there for her to mop up her tears and give her advice – and I know from experience she'd be there for me, too."
Janine, 15, Leeds

It's important for the balance to be right in friendships, especially when it comes to support and advice. We all have our own problems, and we all need someone to turn to at those times. So as well as feeling confident enough to trust your friend to help you out, you also need to make it clear that you're available for her whenever she needs you.

LENDING AND HELPING

Wrong:
"My mate's so much luckier than I am. She has fantastic clothes, posh make-up, and loads of CDs and stuff. So I know she doesn't mind when I borrow things. I've had some of her belongings for ages, but she obviously doesn't mind because she doesn't say anything – she's good like that."
Ashleigh, 14, Harlow

This is a real case of taking advantage. Ashleigh is getting the perks of a generous friend, without giving anything in return. Ashleigh needs to start giving and stop taking if she expects this relationship to last.

Right:
"My mate Sara is dead clever – she gets top marks in all of her classes. I get really stuck with maths and geography, but Sara's great because she always offers to help me out. Although I can't do the same for her, I try to make it up for her by making her thank you cards or cooking her dinner." Christina, 16, Peterborough

Once again Christina and Sara are putting an equal amount of effort into their friendship. They're making sure they both work at the relationship. They realise they can't offer the same things, but they balance this out by giving each other what they can.

TIPS TO MAINTAIN YOUR FRIENDSHIP

Want to keep your friendship in tip-top condition? Then follow these handy hints.

1 Say thanks
Want to say thank you to your friend? Why not invite her over for the evening and give her a night of pampering? Light some candles, stick on some ambient music, and get to work transforming her look with a manicure, pedicure, facial and makeover.

2 Make the effort
Make sure you both put an equal amount of effort into your friendship – if she's calling you all the time, make sure you find the time to call her. Or why not surprise her by sending her a card or letter?

3 Involvement
It's important to always make your friend feel included. You don't have to live in one another's pockets, but if you're having a big girly night out make sure you always invite *all* of your friends. Don't leave anyone out!

4 Compromise
Make sure you compromise once in a while. It's important to stand up for yourself, and to do things that interest you, but if you're asking your friend to get involved then you need to make sure you sometimes do things that are good for her, too.

5 Remember important dates!
How awful would you feel if your best buddy forgot your birthday, or if she forgot to ask you how

your big exam went? Terrible, right? So make sure you always remember stuff that's important to her. And if you've got a bad memory, make sure you write it in your diary. There's no excuse!

Chapter 7

ARE YOU A GOOD FRIEND?

We all know the stuff we love and hate about our mates. But have you ever sat back and thought about the type of friend you make? You may be really loving, caring and considerate or perhaps you're totally annoying (yeah, right). Take our in-depth test and find out how you rate as a mate.

TASK 1: WHAT ARE YOU LIKE?

1. Study the list of words over the page. Pick five that you think describe you best.
2. Next ask a friend to do the same. Remember to make a note of your answers.

Happy
Funny
Deep
Thoughtful
Spiritual
Crazy
Loyal
Likeable
Polite
Loud
Quiet
Outspoken
Shy
Unpredictable
Impatient
Self-centred
Bossy
Committed
Head-strong
Carefree

Now add up your score.

a Add up the point score of the words you picked: Happy (1.5), Funny (2), Deep (0.5),

Thoughtful (2.5), Spiritual (2.5), Crazy (2), Loyal (1.5), Likeable (2), Polite (2.5), Loud (0.5), Quiet (2.5), Outspoken (0.5), Shy (1), Unpredictable (2), Impatient (0.5), Self-centred (1), Bossy (1), Committed (1.5), Headstrong (1.5), Carefree (1)

b Tot up the point score for your mate's answers too.

c Look at the words you and your friend chose. If all of your answers are the same, score 3 points, if none are the same, score 1 point, if two or three words are the same, score 2 points.

d Make a note of your total point score for this section.

3 Take a look at the second list of words overleaf. Now pick two things you think you give your mates in your friendship.

4 Once again, ask your friend to do the same – what are their two main reasons for hanging out with you?

A good laugh
Companionship
Loyalty
Trust
A top social life
Care and advice
Guidance
Education
Commitment
Everything!

Now add up your score.

a As before, add up the point score of the answers you picked: A good laugh (2), Companionship (1.5), Loyalty (1), Trust (1.5), A top social life (2), Care and advice (2.5), Guidance (0.5), Education (0.5), Commitment (2.5), Everything! (1)

b Tot up the point score for your mate's answers.

c Look at the words you and your friends chose. If your two choices of words are the same, score 3 points, if none are the same, score 1 point, if one is the same, score 2 points.

d Make a note of your total point score for this section. ☐

Now add up the combined total of both of your scores, and make a note of it in this box. ☐

TASK 2: HOW YOU BEHAVE

Take a careful look at the following scenarios – and the responses outlined. Choose which you think best describes the way you are most likely to respond to your friends.

1 Your friend has just split up with her boyfriend of nine months. She is absolutely devastated. Her mum gives you a call to see if you can cheer her up. What do you do?

a You go round, storm into her room, demand that she pulls herself together, then tell her you're off to the cinema. If she wants to come she will, if not you can't bear to see her moping.

b You go round, bound into her room, trying to suppress your giggles when you spot your buddy sprawled across the bed surrounded by love letters and photos. You give her a hug, tell her there are plenty more fish in the sea, then spend the next hour telling hilarious stories in an attempt to get her smiling again.

c You pop around to see your friend. You tell her how awful her break-up must be, and spend five minutes listening to her tales of sadness. You then start talking about your own problems in a bid to distract her from her own misery (and to make it 100% clear she doesn't have the monopoly on sadness).

d You go to the shop first and buy a huge tub of ice cream, a selection of choccie bars, a couple of mags and a girly video. When you get there you sit with her for hours while she cries her heart out, before leaving her with the big stash of goodies.

e You agree to visit your friend, and call her first to tell her to get dressed. Then you take her for a walk in the park so she has a chance to get out of the house, clear her head and pour her heart out to you. You know she's not going to feel happy straight away – but you make it clear you'll be there for her whenever she needs to talk.

2 You and your friend decide to go shopping together. She wants to buy a nice dress to impress her crush at the end-of-term party. She has her heart set on a tight red mini-dress. The trouble is, it's really not flattering. You know she's going to be really upset if you tell her it looks disgusting. What do you do?

a There's no way you can tell her. So you smile, tell her she looks cool, and then leave the shop with her brand new purchase. You do feel a bit guilty, but when you see how happy she is you can't bear to tell her different. In the back of your mind you're willing her mum to tell her the truth when she sees her in it.

b You tell her she looks like a bag of spuds in an ankle sock. So what if the truth hurts? It would definitely hurt more if she left her house dressed like that.

c You um and ah, and persuade her to try on a different (more flattering) dress. You then spend the next 30 minutes persuading her to buy the second dress. You think of hundreds of reasons like: it's a classic, it'll never date, you look soooo sophisticated, etc. . . . In the end she's convinced. It's been hard work, but she's happy because she thinks she's made the decision all on her own.

d You tell her you're not sure it's quite her. While she's trying something else on you decide to give the dress a shot. It looks much better on you, so before she has a chance to complain you tell her you're going to buy it, before legging it to the cashier.

e Start laughing. You don't mean to, but she really looks ridiculous. You apologise for being tactless when she rips the dress off in a huff. You know she'll forgive you – especially when you find her a nicer dress that suits her more.

3 You and your best buddy decide to go to the cinema. You've just seen an ad for a new chick flick that you want to see. Trouble is, your friend has been talking about another film that she's been gagging to see for ages. When you get there what do you choose to do?

a Flip a coin – the choice of the film is down to chance, and you've agreed to see the 'loser's' film next week as well.

b Let her see her film. You'd much rather she was happy – you can always see the film you want to see when it comes out on video.

c Demand you see your film – it looks a million times better than the one she wants to see anyway.

d Play the martyr – you tell her you'll see her film if you must, but you make it completely clear you're compromising for her. You know there's a chance if you whinge enough she may just give in.

e Shrug your shoulders and get her to make the decision.

4 You're getting changed in the dressing-room for football when you overhear another gang of girls talking. They're gossiping about your best buddy – and telling a made-up story about her copping off with a gross boy. What do you do?

a Sneak out – you don't want to upset anyone.

You decide not to tell your friend – she'd be gutted if she knew.

b Start laughing – then tell them they've got it all wrong. She was really snogging the most popular boy in school. So what if it's not true? If they're going to gossip about your buddy you can at least make sure she comes out on top.

c Tell the gang to stop gossiping about your friend – especially when they've got their facts wrong. You tell them you're going to tell your buddy – if only to get them worried.

d Hide away and listen to what they've got to say. Then ask your mate what she would do if she ever heard anyone talking about *you*. Her response will make up your mind about what you're going to do.

e You ignore them. So what if they're gossiping? It's got nothing to do with you.

5 Your friend has started copying you. Every time you buy a new top she'll run out and buy the same one. She's even copied your haircut, the way you say stuff, and your likes and dislikes. It's driving you bonkers. What do you do?

ARE YOU A GOOD FRIEND?

a Tell her she's stupid. It's time she got her own life.
b Laugh it off – who cares if she's copying you? You're the original!
c Say nothing. It's obviously a compliment, and you'd really offend her if you did say anything.
d Sit her down and talk to her. You tell her you're flattered, but it's not quite right. You tell her she doesn't need to copy you to be your friend – before adding that you liked her before because she was so different.
e You spot a hideous orange fluffy coat in the shops. You tell her you've just bought it, even though you haven't. You know she's going to run out and buy the same coat, which means you'll get the last laugh.

Now add up your score . . .
  1 a 1 **b** 4 **c** 2 **d** 5 **e** 3
  2 a 5 **b** 1 **c** 3 **d** 2 **e** 4
  3 a 3 **b** 5 **c** 1 **d** 2 **e** 4
  4 a 5 **b** 4 **c** 3 **d** 2 **e** 1
  5 a 1 **b** 4 **c** 5 **d** 3 **e** 2
and make a note of your score in this box: ☐

TASK 3: HOW YOU FEEL

Now look at the next set of scenarios. This time you must select the answer closest to the way each situation would make you feel.

1 Your friend has had a big row with one of your mutual friends. She's really upset and reckons this other girl has been well out of order. Are you:
a Amused?
b Angry?
c Upset?
d Understanding?
e Unemotional?

2 You've had a big bust-up with your best friend about a boy you both fancy. Are you:
a Devastated?
b Forgiving?
c Stubborn?
d Confused?
e Not bothered?

3 You and your friend both audition for the role of Sandy in your school production of *Grease*. She gets it. Are you:

- **a** Jealous?
- **b** Angry?
- **c** Delighted?
- **d** Pleased but disappointed?
- **e** Amused?

4 You've just found out your best friend's boyfriend has been cheating on her. You decide to confront him. Are you:

- **a** Disappointed?
- **b** Gutted?
- **c** Annoyed?
- **d** Aggressive?
- **e** Glad she's broken up with the creep?

5 You're mucking about with your friend in the playground. Your new boyfriend walks past, just as she shoves you into another lad. Are you:

- **a** Embarrassed?
- **b** Amused?

c Annoyed?
d Upset?
e Not bothered?

Now add up your score . . .
  1 a 4 **b** 1 **c** 5 **d** 3 **e** 2
  2 a 5 **b** 3 **c** 1 **d** 2 **e** 4
  3 a 1 **b** 2 **c** 5 **d** 3 **e** 4
  4 a 2 **b** 5 **c** 3 **d** 1 **e** 4
  5 a 5 **b** 4 **c** 1 **d** 2 **e** 3

and make a note of your score in this box:

YOUR CONCLUSION

To find out if you are a good friend you need to tot up your total score. To do this all you need to do is add up all the scores for each section.

Write that total here:

Now check out what type of friend you are:

55 and above

You are a genuinely nice and caring person and will go out of your way to help other people. Your friends really love you because you are so adorable. You are selfless, generous, supportive and emotional. You are very sensitive and hate to see other people upset or unhappy. You make a great friend because you are so interested in making other people happy – your best buddy's happiness makes your day.

But be careful. A lot of people you meet may try to take advantage of your niceness (especially as you get older), using you to get what they want. So although it's lovely to be nice, you must make sure that nobody's taking advantage of you. It's also worth remembering that you do have to think of yourself sometimes – so if you really don't want to do something, don't do it. You are completely within your rights to be selfish from time to time, and your mates will respect you for this.

46 – 54

You love life. You're completely happy-go-lucky, and love to have a giggle. You have a real energy about you – and everyone who comes into contact with you is infected by your pure energy for life. You really want your friends to enjoy their lives – so if they're feeling down you do your utmost to get a smile back on their faces.

Your friends can't get enough of you because you're so fun to be around. But from time to time we all need a break. It's impossible to be the life and soul of the party 24/7. It's OK to feel down sometimes (in fact, in a weird way, it's sometimes quite nice), so don't try to make a joke out of every situation. And remember, sometimes it's not appropriate to laugh – your friends may not be amused if you're cracking jokes at their misfortune. Save your laughs for the rest of the time – and keep on enjoying life.

36 – 45

You are a fantastic friend. You read situations – and people – really well, which is why you're good mate material. You know when to laugh, when to cry, when to snigger, and when to stand up for yourself. You have a lot of strong opinions, and if you think you or your mates are being unfairly treated you won't think twice about fighting back.

Your pals are totally important to you. In fact, you value friendship above most other things.

Which is why you work so hard at it. You know it's important to put effort in, and to be there for your friends. But you also understand the value of having a good laugh. Your friends learn a lot from you – which is why you're so popular.

21 – 35

You put a lot of trust in your friends, who are an essential part of your life. It's important for you to have mates for advice, understanding, companionship and loyalty. You'd give your friends the world – as long as you get the same treatment in return.

You want your friends to be as devoted to you as you are to them. You have such high standards, and worry about your friends' loyalty so much, that you often end up feeling let down and disappointed. You don't mean to depend on your mates so much – and your worrying often gets in the way of you having fun. Remember, you make a great friend, so stop worrying and start enjoying!

20 or less

You have rather a bad case of being little miss bossy boots! You love to take control of situations, and get frustrated if people don't want to do what you want to do. You don't mean to be bossy or controlling – in fact, you're sure you're helping your friends out by making decisions for them. But everyone likes to be independent at times, which is why you need to let people make their own minds up. You can't wrap them up in cotton wool forever!

Remember, not everyone wants to do what you want to do. If you try too hard at organising everyone's lives you'll just drive them away – so learn to relax, have fun and make some mistakes once in a while.

SECTION 2
FRIENDSHIP DILEMMAS

Chapter 8

YOUR FRIENDSHIP PROBLEMS

Every month on *Bliss* we get hundreds of letters from readers who are having problems with their mates. From friends who are just plain nasty to mates who are too possessive or care too much.

What's interesting is that no matter who you are, no matter where you're from, everyone seems to go through the same ups and downs with their buddies. It's kind of reassuring to know that we all experience the same things – because it means we'll all be able to sort our dilemmas out. Here's a look at five of the most common problems we hear about.

The problem:
I feel left out

Dear Bliss,

I have been mates with my best friend since we were eight. We've been through everything together, and I really don't know what I'd do without her. The trouble is, she's started hanging out with another group of girls, and I'm feeling really left out. It's not that she doesn't invite me – she always does – but my mum won't let me hang out at the places they all go out to. At school on Mondays they always talk about their 'great weekends' and all the fun stuff they get up to, and I don't know what they're on about. I'm worried my best friend will start to enjoy life without me. After all, why would she want to hang out with a boring square like me? Jane, 15, Swansea

The advice:

It's always hard to watch your friends going out and having fun without you – especially when you really want to join in. It sounds to me like your friend really does want to involve you, and is probably aware that you may feel left out. You should try telling her how you feel. If she understood exactly how sad this was making you, I'm sure she would make the effort to spend some weekends at places your mum was happy for you to go to.

You should also try talking to your parents. If their restrictions are preventing you from socialising with your friends, you could sit down together and try to work out some sort of compromise. They are just looking after you by placing restrictions on where you can and can't go – but they are probably unaware of how miserable these are making you.

It sounds to me like you still have a friend. Don't resent her for having new mates – it gives you plenty of new stuff to talk about. Just be honest and try to do as much together as possible – with a genuine friend like you there's no way she'd consider you to be boring or square, or even think about moving on.

Of course there is a small chance your friendship may have come to a natural end. It would be really worth trying to find more friends, and doing other things, so you don't end up relying heavily on one person. It's a good idea to make friends in those places your parents are happy for you to go to. That way you won't run into any problems.

The problem:
My mate's going bonkers!

Dear Bliss,

I am really worried about my friend. We have known each other for four years, and throughout that time have always been really close. We liked the same music, were into the same things, and had a top time hanging out together. But recently she seems to have changed.

She's started hanging out with a different bunch of girls. When she's with them she bunks off school, smokes, snogs loads of boys and generally tries to make herself look cooler. If I'm about she'll try to make me look stupid by calling me names like Plain Jane and Boring Brenda. Not only is it upsetting me, but I reckon she's going to get herself into big trouble. What should I do?
Maya, 14, Hastings

The advice:

The most important thing is that your mate doesn't lead you astray. There's no point in you getting into trouble for your friend. If you still value your friendship you should try talking to her. Don't try to do this in front of her new mates because she'll get embarrassed and defensive – which means she'll probably end up taking it out on you. So get her one-on-one and tell her you're worried about her. You also need to point out that you're not going to hang about just so she can take the mick out of you.

Her reaction will dictate what you do next. If she's horrible, abusive or just ignores you it's up to you to walk away. There are plenty of other girls out there who would value a friend like you – you don't deserve to be picked on. And she'll probably learn her lesson the hard way when her parents or teachers find out what she's been up to – or when she fails to live up to her new mates' 'coolness'. However, if she does listen to you then stick with her. She may just be going through a rebellious time, which means she's really going to need a friend she can trust when her new world comes crashing down around her . . . which it will!

The problem:
They're bitching about me!

Dear Bliss,

I am so gutted, I really don't know what to do. I've just found out that the group of girls I hang out with have been bitching about me. Not just one or two of them . . . the whole lot. I can totally believe this because I've seen them do it to a couple of other friends, too. But even they've joined in. Please tell me what to do? Should I put up with their bitching? Or maybe I should bitch back? I'm so confused.

Sam, 16, London

The advice:

It's a sad fact of life that some girls really do love to bitch about their friends. And, when it does happen, it's a harsh lesson about the people in life you can really trust. Let's face it, if they were real, genuine mates they wouldn't talk about you like this. Real friends don't have bad things to say about their mates – after all, why do you choose to hang out with someone you don't really like?

My advice to you is to walk away. You've just

found out you can't really trust these girls, and if they've done it once they'll do it again. They'll be dead embarrassed when they find out that you know what they've been saying. If they do have a sensitive bone in their bodies they'll probably try and make up with you. If they do, it's important to make it clear how you feel. It's really their loss to miss out on a good friend. And, if they do carry on like this, they're going to end up very sad and lonely. So don't be in a hurry to hang out with them again – you'll soon make new mates who would never stab you in the back like that.

The problem:
We're growing apart

Dear Bliss,
My best friend and I have been mates since we were born – our mums were best friends, and we were born within a few months of each other, so they kind of brought us up like sisters. We see each other every weekend because that's when our mums see each other. The thing is, it's really obvious to us that we're growing apart. We barely have anything to talk about now because our lives

are completely different – and we definitely don't tell each other secrets. We really have become best friends in name only. I know she feels the same but I don't want to hurt her feelings – or Mum's.
Guilty, 17, Oxford

The advice:

First of all, you really don't need to feel guilty. It's perfectly natural for friends to grow apart. The fact that you're both concerned about each other's feelings shows that you still really care about each other. It's not surprising that you've very little in common. Just because you've grown up together doesn't mean you'll necessarily be into the same things.

It sounds like you probably don't need to make any big decisions with your mate to end your status as best friends, but you do need to explain how you feel to your mum. Have a chat with her and tell her how you feel – she'll probably agree to let you give the weekly visits a miss. If you're not forced to see one another you'll gradually drift apart. If your mums are best friends it's inevitable you'll still meet up from time to time. But then, when you do see each other, you'll actually have something to talk about.

The problem:
My mum hates my mate

Dear Bliss,

I've got a really big problem – my mum hates my best mate. We've been friends ever since we started secondary school, but Mum's convinced she's a bad influence on me. She's banned her from our house, never lets me go out to parties with her, and is really rude to her if she ever calls the house. I'm not going to stop being friends with her, but I desperately want to get Mum off my back. What should I do?
Charlie, 14, Ilford

The advice:

This is a tricky one. You need to come to some sort of compromise with your mum. Start by trying to work out why your mum doesn't like this girl. Have your grades dropped since you started hanging out together? Or have you been bunking off school or lying to your parents? Can you see any way in which your mate could be seen as a bad influence?

If you can answer "yes" to any of these it really is up to you to change things. Your mum is never going to approve if this is still happening – so make the effort to pick up your grades and stop playing up. If she spots signs of improvement she'll become more relaxed towards your friend.

If you genuinely can't see a problem then you need to start a plan of re-education. Tell your mum you're still great friends – and it would mean a lot to you if your mum would get to know your friend more. The best way to do this is to arrange a meeting between your mum and your buddy so your mum can see why she's good for you. If she's such a good friend this'll be a breeze. And make sure you keep reminding your mum why she's a great mate – e.g. she really looks out for me/she did the sweetest thing/she really cheered me up/she helped me with my coursework. Your mum just wants you to be safe and happy – which is why you have to prove your friend also wants the same things.

Chapter 9

WHEN YOU MAKE MISTAKES

Nobody likes to admit when they've done something wrong. Think about how many times you've claimed "It's not my fault". It's the hardest thing in the world to stand back, take a look at yourself and say, "Oops, I messed up". And, let's face it, we all do mess up from time to time. But as long as you can recognise when you've made a mistake you're OK – because then you've got a chance to do something positive about it. Things only go seriously wrong if you make the same mistakes again and again, or if you wrap yourself up in a little bubble and try to pretend you're perfect.

So, take a look at your relationships with your friends. If there is something wrong it's easier to sort out by taking a look at your own mistakes. It could be that you're making bad judgements, even though all you're actually trying to do is be really nice. So don't feel bad if you do think you've messed up. Just take this opportunity to sort yourself out (before anyone else even notices)!

The crime: You are accused of trying too hard

Trying too hard is a very weird thing. After all, we all love to think that people think we're special, and that they'd do anything for us. A certain amount of effort is essential. As we've seen earlier in the book if you don't bother putting any effort into your friendships you're likely to lose your mates – after all, you can't expect someone else to put the effort in and for you to sit back and enjoy it. However, as with all annoying things in life, the reverse of this is also true. Try too hard and you'll end up stinking of desperation – and that's not pretty for anyone!

So how do you define trying too hard? I guess

the best thing is to take a look at what you consider to be a 'normal' amount of effort. So, normal is:

- Calling your friends as much as they call you.
- Making your friend feel 'special' once in a while with a funny gift or cute card.
- Remembering important dates for your friend – like their birthday or exam days.
- Doing things your friend enjoys once in a while, even if you hate doing it.
- Meeting up regularly.

Therefore, you could say trying too hard is:

- **Calling your friend every day, at least three times a day.**
  It's absolutely essential to give your mates some space. They'll feel smothered and restricted if you go on at them too often – and what the hell would you talk about anyway?
- **Being overly generous – too many gifts, cards and special treats.**
  You run the risk of upsetting the balance in the friendship if you go out of your way constantly to make her feel special. She may

start feeling guilty, or start resenting the gifts. They'll also lose their impact – there's not really anything special about something that happens every day.

- **You'd be right to remember important dates – but remember every minute detail and your friend may worry she's being stalked.** The key is not to get obsessive. Your friend will really appreciate you remembering to wish her luck before her Grade 5 piano exam, but will be rather alarmed if you congratulate her on the third anniversary of the day her period started.

- **Only ever doing things your friend wants to do.** If you always give in, never have any desire to do something on your own, or have a complete inability to make a decision you may as well take a paintbrush and slap the letters d–o–o–r–m–a–t across your forehead. Of course it's great to make her happy – but she'd probably like to return the favour . . . The granny cliché, giving is as good as receiving, is actually true. So don't be selfish by being too kind!

- **Wanting to hang out *all* the time.**
  Once again, this comes down to giving each other space. You don't need to see each other every spare minute to prove that you're best friends – best buddies will always be just that, even if they live on opposite sides of the world.

So there's your basic definition of 'trying too hard'. The sad thing about this crime is that you only ever do it to try and make your friend happy – but by doing it you're running the risk of achieving the complete opposite. So try to consider your own needs and desires, as well as your friend's, and don't be scared to think "me, me, me" once in a while.

The crime: You are accused of being bossy

We all know there's nothing worse than being told what to do all the time. It's one of the reasons for getting so annoyed with your parents and your teachers – you just want to be left to make up your own mind, or do your own thing, from time to time. Which is why being bossy is a big crime to friendship. If you constantly tell your friends where to go, what to do, what to wear, how to get their hair cut, who they should talk to, how to do stuff, what's cool and what's rubbish, then you're on a treadmill to an argument. Sooner or later your mates will tell you where to stick your bossy ways and make sure they never ask for advice when you're in the vicinity.

It's true that your bossiness is probably meant in the best possible way – your attempt at looking out for your friends, keeping them safe, and advising them on the 'best' course for their lives. But really, can you imagine how annoyed you'd get if someone kept telling you what to do?

Learn to bite your tongue and let your friends experiment and make mistakes with their own lives – they'll thank you for it in the end.

The crime: You are accused of laziness

Uh-oh, this girl's got couch potato syndrome. Nobody really wants a lazy mate. It's just too frustrating to listen to them whine "can't be bothered", "too tired" or "don't want to go out" all the time.

In fact, if you're the type of lazy person who always wants their friends to come over and see them, you're destined to lose out on friendships and good times. If you're unenthusiastic, or can't be bothered to make any effort, your friends will soon lose interest in you. After all, what are they getting out of this friendship? So if you do value your mates, and want to be involved, then get up off your bum and start making the effort. You never know, you might even enjoy it.

The crime: You are accused of trying to be liked by everyone

It's no secret that all people are different. Some people love to be lovely, some people love to be grumpy. Some people only need a few best friends, some people need a big gang. The point is that in our lives and in our friendships we all want different things. Which is why – however great you are – you are not going to be best buddies with everyone you meet, and neither should you want to be. If you try to get everyone to like you you'll have to play a funny game where you are different things to different people – which means you never get to have fun playing yourself! You'd have to be girly with one group, sexy with another, bitchy with some friends and considerate to others. It's virtually impossible to maintain this many personalities, and you're being incredibly cruel to yourself. There's also a chance that your friends may cotton on to your multiple personas and accuse you of being false, or force you to make a choice between different friends – whatever happens someone is bound to get hurt (probably you).

So decide what you want out of your friendships and go for that – it really is about quality, not quantity.

The crime:
You are accused of being possessive

This crime fits neatly alongside the crime of 'trying too hard'. The possessive friend can be a big fat pain. She doesn't mean to – and she'd be devastated if she knew what a pain she was being – but she's completely insecure and feels the need to 'own' her mate. Almost as if she was dating them.

There are a few ways to identify whether or not you're being possessive:
- You get annoyed if your friend sees other people without you.
- You expect to be invited everywhere she goes.
- You'd have a go at her if she told somebody else a secret, but not you.
- You think she's a bad friend when she decides to have a night in on her own.
- You try to jeopardise her other friendships.

Possessiveness is a very unhealthy emotion in any relationship, and if you start feeling that way you need to get it sorted. There are loads of reasons why it's important to give your friends space. Here are a few:
- If you see each other all the time you never have anything to talk about. Having time apart allows you to do new things, then share your gossip afterwards.
- If you spend all your time with one person your life experience will be limited – new people can lead us to try out new things, which we can then introduce to our other friends.

- You can't put all your eggs in one basket. If you rely heavily on one person, what will you do if they're not there? If your friend goes on holiday who will you talk to, or hang out with, or have fun with? And that's only for a couple of weeks . . . what would you do if she moved away forever?
- Everyone needs some sort of breathing space. The minute we start to feel claustrophobic and trapped we start rebelling. So it's bye bye friendship, hello loneliness.

So try your hardest to avoid the pitfalls of possessiveness. The best way to do this is to make sure you are not dependent on one person. Try and make new friends and develop different interests. It won't stop you having best friends, but it will broaden your horizons.

/ Chapter 10

WHEN FRIENDSHIP TURNS SOUR

A ruined friendship is one of the worst things that can ever happen to us girls. It's a horrible time and it makes us question so many things. Is it me? Am I a cow? Am I boring? How will I live without a great mate like her? Why did she want to hurt me? What's wrong with me? Will I ever find a friend again? There are so many questions – and definitely not enough answers.

The reason it hurts so much is because our best mates mean the world to us. We spend time with them and trust them with our secrets. We essentially give part of ourselves to them – and we expect them to treasure that. Discovering you were wrong, or that your mate didn't value your friendship as much as you did, hurts. But you have to remember one thing – you will get over it. At first that seems like a stupid thing to say – how could you ever get over something that big? But every day the pain will ease and you'll start feeling happier again. Still don't believe it? Then why not read 15-year-old Kaycee's story?

Kaycee's story

"Er, hi . . . you're new here aren't you?" I swung round and nervously smiled. Standing in front of me was the prettiest girl I'd ever seen. She was grinning from ear to ear and stuck her hand towards mine. "Don't be nervous," she said. "It's really not that scary here. I'm Donna. You can hang out with me if you like."

Like? I was over the moon. I was dreading being the new girl at the school. My family had just moved from London, and we were all trying to settle into our new lives here in Newcastle. My friends were a million miles away and I was terrified. Donna saved me from a fate worse than death – being Nora no mates.

Donna was the most popular girl in school. Everyone loved her, and I loved being her friend. It wasn't long before we were inseparable. We laughed at the same stuff, both fancied the pants off Craig David, and told each other our innermost secrets. We had a great group of friends. Although I still kept in touch with my mates in London, I had stopped missing them. I was totally happy.

One weekend Donna's older brother, Ben, was throwing his eighteenth birthday party. We were so excited, and spent the whole of Saturday getting ready. Not only were our parents letting us go alone, but there were going to be older boys there. "I'm so glad you're going to be with me tonight," Donna said. "You're so gorgeous and popular – I wouldn't want to be with anyone else." I couldn't believe it – Donna thought I was gorgeous and popular. "Shut up," I laughed. "Thanks for inviting me. You're my best mate in the world – I'd be gutted if we didn't get to party together." We had a big hug and started giggling. This was going to be the best night of our lives.

Party time

Finally Donna and I were ready and we headed off to the party. We walked into the hall and the music was banging. Donna spotted her brother and raced off to say "hello", leaving me by the door.

"Hi. I'm Declan," a voice boomed behind me. I looked over my shoulder and my jaw hit the ground. Declan was the most gorgeous boy I'd seen in my life. I was in love. We started chatting, and hit it off instantly. An hour later, Donna reappeared.

"Where've you been?" I asked. Donna just giggled and pointed to her brother and a group of his friends. She was stumbling all over the place. I moved to put my arm around her. "Have you been drinking?" I asked.

"Yeah . . . my brother's got some Thunderbird. Fancy some?"

"No thanks," I replied. "Don, have you met D–?" Before I could finish my introduction Donna was off, muttering "Boring cow!" as she disappeared into the crowd. I couldn't believe it. What was up with Donna?

Declan ignored her and asked me to dance. I was really upset, but what could I do? I wasn't going to make a scene in front of everyone – especially Declan. While I was dancing Declan told me he really fancied me. I gave him my number and we agreed to go out. He was just moving in to give me a kiss when I spotted Donna throwing up in the corner. "Look, Declan," I smiled, "I'm really sorry, but I need to help my friend."

"I agree," he nodded. "But let's go out soon."

My heart was racing as I moved towards Donna. But my excitement disappeared when I saw the state she was in. I picked her up and dragged her to the toilets to clean her up. A rubbish way to end an almost perfect evening.

The morning after

Donna had the hangover from hell the next day. She couldn't remember anything, but had an awful feeling she'd snogged this gross lad called Steven.

"Don't worry," I laughed. "I'd be more worried about the fact you called me a boring cow."

The smile drained from Donna's face. "I did what? God, I'm so sorry. I really didn't mean it – must have been the booze. Forgive me?"

"Of course," I laughed. "Evil booze, eh?"

"So, I saw you were talking to Declan," Donna said slowly.

"Oh . . . see, you do remember something! He didn't mention he knew you. He's lovely though. We're going on a date," I grinned.

I left Donna to sleep off her hangover and headed home. Later that day I got a text from Declan. "Wnt 2 C a film 2nite?" How could I refuse an offer like that?

Weird rumours

The date was amazing, and Declan was a perfect gent – he didn't even try it on with me. I floated into school the next day and told Donna what had happened.

"Oh, thanks so much for calling me to let me know," she glared.

"Oh, sorry Don," I said, "I just thought you'd need your sleep."

"Yeah, right," she replied.

Donna didn't say another word to me that day. Or the next. By Wednesday I was really worried.

"Look, Donna, what's going on?" I asked.

Donna snarled, "Look. Declan's a friend of Ben's – and you're messing him about. I heard about you and Steven at the party – everyone has – it's disgusting. I can't believe you two-timed someone as lovely as Dec."

"What the hell are you talking about?" I demanded. "It was you who snogged Steven."

"Yeah . . . but it was you who slept with him. I can't keep this a secret from Declan any more – I'm going to tell him."

And she did.

My mind was reeling. I'd never even spoken to Steven let alone . . . no, it was just too horrible.

I tried to call Declan but he'd always press busy on his mobile. Donna was refusing to talk to me, and everyone was gossiping about me at school. Within a week I'd lost everything.

The truth

On the Friday I was leaving school on my own when Cat, a quiet girl in one of my classes, came running up to me. "Er . . . I'm Cat," she whispered. "I need to talk to you. I know what's going on."

"Oh, you mean you've heard the rumours," I said bitterly.

"Of course . . ." she stopped. "Look the thing is, I know that's exactly what they are. Rumours."

We sat down on the wall outside the school and Cat told me everything. I couldn't believe it.

It turned out that Cat had been Donna's best friend before I arrived at the school but, just before I'd arrived, they'd fallen out. Cat had started dating Ben, Donna's brother. Donna had been so jealous she told Ben – and the rest of the school – that Cat had cheated on him.

"I think she's doing the same to you," Cat frowned. "What was the name of the boy you went out with? I bet it was the lad she asked out last year – he turned her down and she was gutted."

And sure enough, it was.

Confrontation

I didn't know what to think. Why hadn't Donna told me about this mystery friend, Cat? Why hadn't she told me she fancied Declan? Why did she lie about me and Steven? And why had she turned on me? It was only last week that we'd been talking about what great friends we were – surely Cat must be lying.

But the more I thought about it, the more it made sense. Donna had remembered me talking to Declan, but had pretended not to remember insulting me. She was the only one of our friends at the party, but everyone in school knew about it. And, more importantly, she'd never even asked for my version of the story.

I had to confront her.

Donna was still in school, so I thanked Cat and told her I was going to wait to talk to Donna.

I felt sick as I waited. I didn't want it to be true – and I couldn't understand it. I'd been so lonely without Donna.

Eventually she strolled out of school. She was chatting away to a group of girls, and was grinning. Nice that she wasn't gutted at all. Nice that she could laugh when my whole world was falling apart.

The rest of the girls disappeared and she started walking towards me. Suddenly she saw me, and her smile fell.

"Look, Donna. We need to talk," I said.

"Go on, then . . . I'm waiting," she laughed.

"I know, Donna. I know everything. What I don't understand is why?"

Donna slumped on to the wall beside me. She stared at me with her pretty blue eyes and started crying. "I've been such a bitch," she sniffled. "But I was just so jealous of you."

"Jealous!" I wailed. "You were my friend – not my enemy. Look what you've done to me. To us." Within minutes we were both sobbing our hearts out. I don't know what was worse – thinking Donna hated me, or knowing that she deliberately tried to hurt me.

I had to leave. "I do forgive you, Donna, but I don't think we can be best friends any more," I said quietly. Then I walked away.

Moving on

It turns out Donna decided to do the right thing. She called Declan and told him she'd got it wrong.

I was quite lonely without Donna. I thought about trying to be mates with her again, but it was too hard. I couldn't trust her. When we did see each other we'd always have a laugh, and we'd both remember how good it used to be. But I was too scared to leave myself open to her. Too scared she might get jealous, or try and spite me again.

I never thought I'd find a friend like Donna again. But I was wrong. I became great mates with Cat, the quiet girl in my class and another of Donna's victims.

Donna was still the most popular girl in school – but Cat and I were the happiest.

WHAT TO DO IF YOU FALL OUT WITH A FRIEND

Unfortunately we do fall out with our pals from time to time, for loads of different reasons. Often, you may not even understand why, which can be really frustrating. People handle conflict in various ways, which is why it's important to be prepared.

HOW TO COPE WITH . . . BITCHING

Bitching is really one of the worst ways to fall out with your friend. To find out your pal has been dissing you, disclosing secrets, or has been horrible about you behind your back is one of the worst feelings in the world. It's natural to feel upset and angry. But it's essential not to ignore this. You must ask your friend what's going on.

Remember, there is a chance the person who told you may be a troublemaker, so you must let your friend have her say. If it does turn out that your friend has been bitching about you then it's time to wave goodbye. Don't try to get even by bitching about her (it could really backfire, and it's completely unattractive) just thank your lucky stars that you found out what she's really like. Who wants friends like that anyway?

Sometimes people actually bitch in front of your face. Cheeky or what? But don't get involved in a slagging match. Just walk away and leave her looking the fool. Then, when you're on your own, take your chance to talk to her. She's not likely to play the queen without an audience to egg her on. Tell her how it makes you feel, and make sure she stops it. If she doesn't, it's time to end your friendship. And if the bitching continues, then tell someone like a parent or teacher who can really put an end to her witchy tongue!

HOW TO COPE WITH . . .
BEING IGNORED

OK, picture this. You and your pal have fallen out. It may be about something big or small, but now she's adamant she's not talking to you. She won't answer your calls, she's ignored your texts and emails, and she blanks you when you see her. You really want to sort this out and get back to being friends, but she's making it impossible.

This is a tricky situation. You'll start off eager to solve the problem, but being ignored can make you frustrated and angry. There really is only so much you can do. So make the effort, but if you're still not getting any response it's time to take a break. Maybe she just needs time to cool down.

The best thing to do is to write her a letter explaining how you feel. Make it clear how important your friendship is, but also how frustrating it is that she's not talking to you. Then leave it at that. The ball will really be in her court. If she thinks the friendship is worth salvaging she'll be in touch when she cools off. If she doesn't, you can be confident that you've done everything possible to solve the problem.

HOW TO COPE WITH . . . ARGUMENTS

Uh-oh, this is a toughy. It's always really difficult when you get into a row with your buddy. But the truth is it does happen, and just because you've had a row doesn't mean you can't still be friends. In fact, your friendship may even be stronger after you've ironed out your problems. And, let's face it, if you friendship can survive a row it can survive anything! However, if you handle the row badly, you could end up in serious trouble. So follow these argument "rules"!

- Don't shout if you can help it. It'll cause the argument to escalate into something even bigger.

- Try not to let your emotions get involved. Tears and anger rarely help you talk about your problems rationally.
- Never ever insult your friend. If you end up saying something horrible you can bet your friend will say something horrible back and you'll both end up resenting one another – even if you didn't really mean it. And it'll give you something else to row about. Exactly what you don't need.
- Don't get sidetracked. You've established a problem. The best thing to do is give yourselves a few minutes to calm down and then talk about it – only then will you come up with a resolution or a compromise.
- Make it clear that your friendship is the most important thing. So whatever happens, your priority is to take care of that.
- Bite your tongue. If you do get angry, upset or want to blurt out a load of insults it may be better to walk away. Give yourself space to think about what has upset you. Chances are you'll feel much clearer and far less emotional about it once you've had time to think.

Chapter 11

THREE'S A CROWD

Life's easier when there's just two of you. You find that:
- You never feel left out.
- You don't miss out on any gossip or secrets.
- You can sit next to each other.
- You feel like you're getting undivided attention.
- You can have secret jokes and languages.
- You can get a table 'for two'.

So, what happens when two becomes three?

All of a sudden all the attention you've been getting is divided. There's another person to consider, and it can play havoc with your friendship.

The most important thing is to know how to handle it, because it won't be just the two of you forever.

THE NEW BEST FRIEND

This is probably the hardest third person to handle in your friendship. After all, it's hard not to feel funny when your best buddy gets a friend she values just as much as you. It's more than likely there will be a few problems, but as long as you handle them carefully they won't be problems for long – and you may end up with a great new mate, too.

The problem:
Instead of her telling you all of her secrets, she's now telling new bf (best friend) as well. In fact, they know stuff about each other that you don't know.

The solution:
If you're feeling left out when you're together, just make a point of saying: "Oh, what was that? Think I must have missed that one." Say it lightly

and encourage them to make you feel involved – they probably haven't even noticed they're doing it. It's not essential for you to know the comings and goings of new bf's life, but if you think you could be good friends too, why not set the ball in motion by telling her a little secret of your own?

The problem:
Everywhere you go, new bf comes too. She's not your mate, so you find it hard to relax and be yourself – and you never get a chance to chat about personal stuff.

The solution:
Give your friend a call and tell her how you feel – suggest a night out on your own together. Encourage your friend to see you both separately, so it's no big deal when you do want to have nights alone. And don't get jealous of the time she spends with her new bf either.

The problem:
New bf is trying to steal your friend.

The solution:
As the new girl, she should understand that you

both have a history together and that your friendship will be really important. She'd be a bit of a fool to get in the way of that. Try not to think of each other in terms of competition. You don't need to fight to be a better mate, or compete to spend the most time with your friend. Your friend will like you both for different reasons – so don't try to change that.

Unfortunately, from time to time, it may be the case that the new bf *is* trying to steal your mate. If you feel like new bf is trying to drive you apart you need to sit down with your friend and tell her exactly how you feel. Make it clear that you still really value her friendship and you're not resentful of her new bf, but you do want to make sure that if she ever has any doubts about your friendship she must talk to you straight away. You'll only sort out this problem by being completely honest.

The problem:
You and new bf absolutely hate each other.
The solution:
This is a really tricky one. You don't want to upset your friend by being rude to someone she cares

about – or for her to think she can never have the two of you in the same room together. If you do start getting the hump you'll put your friend in a difficult situation where she is forced to choose between the two of you.

If it really is a problem, you'll have to be mega mature. Ask new bf to meet up for a chat. Try and sort your differences – and be honest, it won't work otherwise. If you can't sort it out, you'll have to agree to disagree. There's no reason why you should both ruin your existing friendships.

Make the effort to see your friend as much as possible separately. But, if you do have to spend time with new bf, make sure you're always on your best behaviour.

BEING THE NEW BF

So what do you do if *you* are the new bf? The key is to be as tactful and considerate as possible. Here are a few pointers:

1 Make a real effort to be nice to old bf. Take an interest in her life, and always be pleasant and chatty.

2 Make sure old bf is invited on nights out.

3 Make sure you give your friend and her old bf space on their own together.

4 If old bf seems a bit protective you must step back and give her time – don't be aggressive or shirty, she just needs some time to adjust.

5 Do not compete. Old bf and your friend have a history – you'll lose out if you make your friend choose.

6 However you don't have to feel chased off by a protective friend. If you feel there's a problem then do speak to her and your new bf, and try to find the best way of dealing with the situation.

THE NEW BOYFRIEND

At various times in your lives, you and your buddy will have boyfriends you want to spend time with. This is completely natural, so don't resent each other for it.

The introduction of another special and important person into your lives obviously means your social time must be split. The rules are pretty much the same as with a new friend – no competition, no hatred, plenty of space – but here are a few more points to help you have happy and harmonious friendships.

IF YOU GET A BOYFRIEND

1. Do not stop seeing your mates in favour of your boyfriend. Reserve a couple of nights a week to see your friends. Not only will that keep your romance fresh and exciting, but it also means you won't become too dependent on him.
2. Remember, boyfriends come and go. Good mates are forever. With that in mind, don't dump your dates with mates just because there's a boy on the scene.
3. Don't try to set your friend up with your boyfriend's mates (unless she asks you to). It's really annoying!
4. Occasionally bring your boyfriend on group nights out – it's important for him to get on with your mates. They shouldn't be competition.
5. Make sure your friend still feels really important – make it clear that she's still the number one girl in your life!

IF YOUR FRIEND GETS A BOYFRIEND

1 Don't be horrible about him. If you feel he really does deserve it then be positive in your criticisms and try to stay well out of any bitching about him.

2 Don't try to get her boyfriend to set you up on dates with his mates – it's annoying for him too!

3 Be happy for your friend – and be sure she knows it. Her boyfriends will be big parts of her life, and your happiness and reassurance will be important to her. And try not to be jealous of their relationship.

4 Make an effort to get to know him – obviously don't flirt though!

5 Insist on a girly night once in a while. She may be a bit soppy and miss her boy, but if they ever split up she'll know she's got some real mates she can turn to.

Chapter 12

THE GREEN-EYED MONSTER

The green-eyed monster is a funny old creature – he rears his ugly head when you least expect it. Like when your best friend gets an A* in English and you get a C, or when your mate bags herself the cutest lad in school. Without even meaning it, you can feel utterly . . . jealous.

Nobody likes to admit when they're jealous of something. After all, our parents teach us at an early age not to be envious of our little friends. So it's not something deliberate we decide to feel when we get older – and we definitely would never admit it. It's just a peculiar emotion that we feel when somebody else gets something, or achieves something, that we really wanted for ourselves.

It's not unusual to feel jealousy towards your friends at certain times in your life because there is a certain amount of competition at school that encourages these feelings. For example, you may feel jealous of your friend if:

- She gets a better grade in class or exams.
- She lands the lead role in the school play.
- She gets a boyfriend.
- You think your friend likes another girl more than you.
- She's experiencing things you've never done.
- You think she's more popular than you.
- She gets her period first!

Any of these things can make us feel those first pangs of jealousy. The key is not to let this emotion eat away at you – resentment may make you nasty or bitter to your mates.

In some ways, a certain amount of competition can be healthy. If you always get beaten in the hundred metres, you'll be even more determined to work harder and win the next race. The same is true of schoolwork. Seeing your mate do better than you can encourage you to try harder.

Jealousy only becomes unhealthy when you let it control how you feel and behave. If you find yourself feeling resentment, bitterness, anger or even wanting revenge because your friend has something you don't, you need to take a look at your friendship. Ask yourself the following questions:

1. Why am I angry?
2. Is she not a great friend?
3. Why am I not happy for my friend?
4. Have I achieved anything that my friend might be jealous of?
5. Is it worth losing my best friend just because I feel jealous?
6. What can I do to stop feeling like this?

Sometimes our envy is increased because our friends seem to be rubbing our faces in their glory. Either they are banging on about how great it feels to have done well, or they are over-sympathising with us for not doing quite as well as them!

"I never thought I'd be envious of my best friend," says Leanne, 15, from Twickenham. *"We*

both did well at school, and were pretty equal. We were great mates – who knew everything about each other.

"But one day we were walking home from school when my friend turned to me and said, 'You know what? I've had more periods than you've got in your timetable.' I was gutted. Firstly because she'd kept it a secret, but secondly because it was something she knew I'd been worried about.

"I guess it's true of all girls that you want to feel like you're growing into a woman – so when your mate beats you to it you can't help feeling a bit gutted. Jealous I guess. But the fact that she was gloating about it made me feel a million times worse."

In a situation like this, you really need to tell your friend how you're feeling. You may find it embarrassing to say: "Er . . . I feel a bit stupid saying this, but I'm jealous. I am happy for you – but I just feel a bit funny about it too. Any chance we can stop talking about it?" But it really is worth it in the end. If your friend doesn't respect that – which most will – then you really need to make it clear that you're going to have to have a bit of space from her until you've got used to it.

Most feelings of envy will amount to nothing. But here are a few do's and don'ts when it comes to handling the green-eyed monster:

Do	Don't
Tell your friend how you're feeling. It will help you come to terms with your emotions.	Get angry or spiteful towards her because she's got something you want. There's no point throwing a tantrum either – it won't help you get what you want.
Be happy for her achievement.	Try to get one back on her by deliberately going after something you know she wants.
Remember all the great stuff you've got going in your life. Some people may be envious of these things, but they don't hold it against you.	Compare yourself with other people. You need to have your own achievements and goals.
Forget about it. There's much more important stuff going on for you to worry about.	Go on about it. There's no point making your friend feel bad by whingeing on about how great she is and how useless you are. It's not her fault!

Chapter 13

COMPATIBILITY

We're always going on about whether or not we're 'compatible' with people – whether it's our friends or our boyfriends. But what is it that makes people compatible? Some of you will argue that it's actually opposites who attract, but the rest of you will think that you've got to be similar in order to be compatible. So which is it?

"I reckon me and my mate are completely compatible – I don't think we'd be such good friends if we weren't. We are just so similar. We both love the Backstreet Boys, we fancy lads that look like Jack Ryder, we love the same food, are massive 'Dawson's Creek' fans, and laugh at the same

jokes. We know that whatever either one of us chooses to do we'll both have a great time because we're into the same things. We never ever argue. It's great."
Evie, 14, Stoke-on-Trent

"To look at me and my best buddy Zara you'd reckon we were enemies – not mates. Nobody believes we're compatible enough to be friends because we're into such different stuff – but we think our differences are what make our friendship so cool. It's just full of surprises.

"She's tall, blonde and a really fluffy girl. I'm a short, scruffy-haired skate kid. She loves Britney, I love Eminem. She loves burgers, I'm a vegetarian. Everything about us is different. But when we get together we talk for hours about what we've been up to – and we've always got loads of questions for each other. We take each other out with our other friends, which is always a weird, but good, experience for both of us. We're the proof that you don't have to be exactly the same to be compatible."
Judith, 15, Walthamstow

So, as you can see, there are no strict rules – Judith and Zara are completely different, but they do have one thing in common which makes their friendship possible; the desire to find out, and learn about, each other's lifestyles.

We all need at least one thing in common with our friends – this is the compatibility needed to make our friendships work. So don't worry if you don't love all of each other's tastes – as long as you can identify at least one thing that you enjoy doing together then you'll be able to maintain a happy friendship. Even if it's just a love of pizza or 'EastEnders'!

THE COMPATIBILITY DILEMMA

Problems with compatibility in friendship usually arise when you both have one personality characteristic, lifestyle preference, or opinion on something which completely contradicts – or clashes with – your friend's.

It's not uncommon for us to have arguments, or differences of opinion, with people. And often these can happen with our friends. That's when it gets hard. You could absolutely adore everything about your friend, except for her opinions on Marilyn Manson! Despite all the stuff you have in common – the things that make you compatible – just one difference can make you spend hours bickering with each other. There are lots of things you may have different opinions on with your friends. For example:

- religion;
- politics;
- relationships (snogging loads of boys is just a bit of fun/snogging loads of boys makes you a slapper);
- racism, or other big issues (cruelty to animals etc. . . .).

Alternatively your differences may be in your preferences for:

- TV shows (soaps are great, they're so true to life/soaps are a load of rubbish, stuff like that never happens in real life);
- music (pop is pants/pop is tops);
- food (I love all meat/I'm a vegan);

- going out (I want to hang out in the park / I want to go to the cinema).

There are a million and one things that you and your friends may disagree on. The thing is, it's OK if it just happens occasionally (a healthy debate never hurt anyone). But if you take the arguments personally, or the disagreements are recurring, then you have a problem.

WHAT TO DO . . .

As you get older you'll find out that we all have differences. It is these differences in personality which make life interesting. Imagine how dull life would be if we all loved each other unreservedly, and agreed on everything. It would definitely be yawnsville.

As you get to know your friends better, you'll start identifying the areas that cause you to fall out. If it is a difference of opinion you both have to be strong and agree to disagree – everyone is allowed their own ideas and opinions, and it is important to respect people for standing by these.

If you have a difference in taste, just avoid

experiencing those things together. If you are a vegetarian who can't stand people eating meat, then you will just have to learn not to go out to dinner with your meat-eating friends. Likewise, if you hate pop music, don't go clubbing with your mates who love it – you don't have to do something just because you think everyone else expects you to. There are still plenty of other things you can do with your friend which you both enjoy.

So here are the no-no's when it comes to differences of opinion:

- Do not try and impose your beliefs or tastes on your friend. Respect their difference of opinion.
- Do not wind them up by deliberately doing, or saying, things you will know will annoy them.

And here are the do-do's:
- Try to understand their point of view. It may teach you something.
- Make the effort to avoid those areas you know you disagree on.

- Enjoy the rest of your friendship. One small disagreement needn't take over your relationship. There are still lots of great things – so make these the focus of your attention.

Chapter 14

JUST GOOD FRIENDS?

We've talked loads about being friends with girls, but what about friendships with those creatures of the opposite sex, otherwise known as boys? Some people are adamant that it's impossible for a girl to just be mates with a boy – insisting that sex, or some kind of flirtatiousness, always gets in the way. But there are many individuals who disagree with this. Look back at Tony and Anne's story in Chapter Four. They're proof that boys and girls can get on fantastically as friends, without any other motives.

MORE THAN FRIENDS

However there are lots of times when friendship can turn into something more. The sad thing is that often it is only one person in the friendship who gets the hots for their mate – which can cause all sorts of problems.

So what do you do when your best buddy tells you they've fallen for you?

SHOULD YOU DATE A MATE?

Whatever happens, it's important not to rush into any sort of sexual relationship with your friend. You're already friends, which means you'll have some strong emotions for one another. These feelings could easily get confused. You need to ask yourself all sorts of questions before agreeing to give it a go. Like:

1. Do I really feel the same?
2. Would I have thought about a relationship if my friend hadn't said anything?
3. Do I love them as a friend, or as a partner?
4. Am I just agreeing so I don't hurt my friend?
5. What will happen to our friendship if a relationship doesn't work out?

The last of these questions is probably the most important of all – what will happen to your friendship if you try and be something more? What happens if it doesn't work out? It's likely that one of you will end up getting hurt – or you may find it hard to go back to being platonic mates after being snogging partners.

If you think it's a gamble worth taking, because the relationship could be fantastic, then you have to be prepared to lose a friend if it doesn't work out.

WHY DID MY FRIEND CHANGE THINGS?

It is not unusual to feel angry with a friend if they tell you they want something more – especially if you don't feel the same. There are lots of reasons for this. You may think:

- You have ruined our friendship. I can't go out with you, but we can't be friends now either because we feel differently about each other.

Or . . .

- You used me and pretended we were friends – just to get close to me.

These are natural reactions. But if you value your friendship it's important to handle these thoughts carefully. There's absolutely no reason for you not to be friends, as long as you sensibly talk it through – and make it clear that nothing is ever going to happen. And it is highly unlikely that your friend has used you to get with you – it's far more likely that they've fallen for you because they know you really well, and love what they know.

THE BRUSH-OFF

OK, so your mate has asked you if you're interested in anything more. You know you're not – so don't string them along, the kindest thing is to be honest. But don't go blundering in with a: "Ugh . . . you're joking aren't you? Don't get me wrong, I like you. But the thought of snogging you makes me want to gag." Instead follow these tips to a pain-free (almost) brush-off.

1 Tell your friend you're really flattered, but you don't feel the same.

2 Make it clear that your friendship is the most important thing in your life, and that a relationship would change that.

3 If it is a girl, and you're not gay, you need to be honest. Tell her that although you don't actually fancy girls, you are completely supportive of her and her sexuality. She's going to need a good friend like you if she is coming to terms with her feelings.

4 It's important to clarify that although you want to be friends, nothing more is ever going to happen. It's cruel to say "things may change", or "maybe in the future". If you don't fancy them now, the likelihood is that you never will.

5 Make sure they don't feel embarrassed. It will have taken your friend a lot of guts to pluck up the courage to say something to you. They need reassurance from you that they haven't just made a complete fool of themselves.

6 Whatever you do, keep this to yourself. Don't go blabbing to other friends about what's happened, or make any sort of joke out of it. You'll really hurt your friend's feelings, and irreversibly damage your friendship.

THE COME-ON

Of course there is a chance that you do feel the same way, and have been willing this to happen ever since you first became mates. If this is the case, make sure you consider the following things before diving in:

1 Before anything else happens talk about what happens if you split up – are you both prepared to gamble your friendship?

2 You will have told each other a lot of stuff as friends (about past partners/secrets etc. . . .). Don't use this against each other in your relationship – especially in arguments.

3 Make the effort to get to know each other again – but as partners. That means lots of dates! Don't make the mistake of thinking you're past that. The early days are great in a relationship and you may feel you've missed out if you don't get that.

4 Try and break the idea of your new relationship gently to your mutual friends. They may be a bit freaked out by you two dating – so no full-on snogfests in front of your buddies.

WHAT HAPPENS IF YOU GET THE CRUSH?

If you get a crush on your friend, but are not sure how they feel about you, it's essential to act carefully. The last thing you want to do is scare your mate off, or jeopardise your friendship, and be left with nothing. Think!

- Has your friend ever given you any reason to think they fancy you?
- Has your friend already got a boyfriend/girlfriend? Or a major crush?
- How will they react?
- Do you really fancy/love them as a partner? Or do you just have strong feelings as a friend? (Could you imagine snogging him?)
- Do you think you'd be better as a couple than as friends?

If you still think it's the right thing to do, be careful. You may end up getting really hurt.

If you're still unsure of what you feel or how to act why not get some professional advice? See the helplines listed on pages 154–5.

Chapter 15

GROWING APART

It's a sad fact in life that not all friendships last forever. It's a natural part of growing up, and experiencing new things. In the process we tend to lose touch with people. But, on the plus side, this gives us even more opportunities to make new friends.

There are lots of reasons why you and a friend may grow apart, like moving away from home or to a different school, or maybe because you've just become really different people. These are usually quite easy situations to handle because the feelings are mutual; you don't really have to worry about hurting someone else's feelings.

The hardest type of growing apart to deal with is when just one of you feels you have outgrown the other.

You know you have grown apart from your friend when:

- You start thinking she's immature.
- You have nothing to talk about.
- She starts annoying you – even though she's not actually doing anything different.
- You would rather spend time with other friends.
- You've stopped confiding in her.
- You're not interested in what she's been doing.
- You don't think you have anything in common any more.

You know your friend is growing away from you when:

- She does more and more without you.
- You have to call *her* all the time.
- You feel like she's changed – you don't really know her any more.
- She never asks how you are.
- Your conversations are stilted.
- You feel left out of her life.

- You don't think you have anything in common any more.

It can be awful to realise your friend is moving away from you. Especially when you still completely value their friendship. The most important thing to remember is that it's not personal.

When you're kids it's easy to be mates – the biggest decisions you have to make are whether to have Marmite or peanut butter sarnies, or whether to watch TV or play on the computer. But as you get older you make different decisions, and start getting to know yourself. You begin to realise that you want certain things in life – and these may be different to what your current friends want. So you seek out people who have the same desires as you – often meeting them in classes or clubs that you are both interested in.

Growing apart from a friend does not mean that you don't like them – often the person moving away will feel guilty because they really do care about their old friend. But they need to stretch their wings and start living their own lives.

So if you feel you're losing a friend, although

you may be sad to lose a good friendship, this is a great time to take a look at your own life and see what you want from it. You're not being left behind – you're just moving in a different direction. A direction that makes *you* happy.

SAYING GOODBYE GRACEFULLY

Unless your friend treats you like a piece of chewing gum on the sole of her shoe, there's no real reason to fall out. Even if you find yourself meeting up less and less, you can still keep each other as friends – but maybe just meeting occasionally. If you make a big fuss about the 'end of a friendship' you risk losing contact altogether. And as you've been good friends, and really cared about each other, that would be a real shame.

So instead of worrying about it, take it face on. Don't sit about moping. Get up, get out, and start making new friends. Have a think about what you're interested in. If you've always wanted to do drama, then use this chance to do just that. Join a drama club and make some new friends with the same interests as you.

If you are feeling lonely without your friend,

talk to your family. They'll help fill the gap until a great new mate comes along – which she will. Whatever you do, don't start harassing your old mate. There's no point sending her letters, calling her house, or hanging around after school for her. If you really have nothing left in common, then it's the best thing for both of you to move on and find friends you'll both enjoy being with.

HELP! SHE WON'T LEAVE ME ALONE!

In many ways it's harder to be the friend moving on – especially if your friend resents it. You'll feel guilty, horrible and selfish, even though you are only doing what is natural.

Although you should never make a big deal about hanging out with new friends, if your old pal is finding it hard to adjust, you really do owe it to her to talk it through. You need to make it clear that it's not personal, you're just doing something new which you happen to enjoy. You need to experience life on your own – you need your independence. Also, make the effort to keep in touch. You may regret losing a mate completely if you don't really need to.

MORE FRIENDS TO COME

One of the best things about life is that we never stop making new friends. Even our grans make new pals at bingo or at parties. We forever find ourselves in situations where we meet new people – parties, at work, through other friends, even in shops. Getting to know new people is great fun, and can teach you a lot (mainly about yourself)! Without even trying, you'll find some fantastic new friends. So don't worry about being alone. Saying goodbye to an old friend is a perfect time to say hello to someone new. If you are still anxious about meeting new people, refer back to Chapter Three: Making Friends.

Chapter 16

BULLYING

Sometimes friendship can go wrong. Not just when you fall out with your mate, or if you don't talk to each other for a week. Far worse than that, sometimes people end up being bullied – often by the people who once called themselves friends.

WHAT IS BULLYING?

Bullying is any act that 'picks on' one person repetitively. There are varying levels of bullying – from name-calling once in a while to constant harassment. A bully's aim is to make their victim as upset, degraded and unhappy as possible.

Bullying can take various forms, such as:

- A big gang picking on weaker kids.
- An individual harassing another individual.

A bully may:

- Call someone names.
- Physically abuse them.
- Spread gossip about someone.
- Try to turn friends against their victim.
- Embarrass their victim in public.
- Use peer pressure to persuade someone to do something they don't want to – like smoking, shoplifting, or even bullying other people.

Bullies use lots of different tactics to get to their victims. The weird thing is, once they're bored of attacking one person they'll often move on to another. It's not really a personal thing – more a demonstration of strength, an assertion of power, or simply a sick pastime. Weirder still, bullies may expect past victims to forgive them – even expecting them to be mates afterwards.

Some bullies get to their victims by humiliating them in front of a crowd – or by encouraging other people to join in. When this happens, the bystanders are almost as guilty as the bully is. They are helping to make this person unhappy.

WHY IS IT BAD?

Victims of bullying will often feel lonely, unhappy, depressed, and unconfident. A person would need a ton of self-confidence in order not be to affected by this sort of behaviour. Often victims of bullying become withdrawn, shy and miserable – some may even take their own lives in order to escape the torment of the bullies.

HOW CAN YOU STOP IT?

If you are being bullied it is absolutely essential to get help. Your parents and teachers can help you sort the problem out – but only if they know about it in the first place.

It's possible that you may be feeling too scared to tell anyone, especially if you have been threatened. But you must. The only way to stop the bully once and for all – and to make sure they don't do it to anyone else – is to tell a person who can help.

Many schools now have specific bullying programmes to help combat this sort of behaviour.

They are experienced in handling these situations and will do everything they can to stop it, and help you.

If you don't feel brave enough to tell an adult, why not confide in a friend? Or try calling one of the helplines on pages 154–5: there are lots of people out there willing to help you, so don't suffer in silence.

A HELPING HAND

If you suspect someone is being bullied you should try to help. It's probably not a good idea to confront the bullies yourself – unless they're friends of yours who may be prepared to listen to what you've got to say. But here are a few things you can do to help:

- Never join in with the bully.
- Talk to the victim. Tell her you can see what's happening, and that you're a friend she can talk to if she needs help.
- Tell your mum or dad or a teacher of your concerns. It's possible the person being bullied may be angry with you for doing this, but it really is the only way to get help.

ARE YOU A BULLY?

Hopefully you can quickly answer 'no' to that question. Bullies are the ringleaders, who initiate an attack on someone. But if you have ever spread gossip, joined in at laughing at someone, or picked on someone to be in with a crowd, you could be guilty of bullying, too.

Bullies are often really insecure people, with a lot of problems of their own. Their victims are usually:

- Easy targets – someone physically weaker, or less aggressive than they are.
- Someone they are jealous of.
- Someone who doesn't fit in, or seems to be different.
- Someone who has wronged them – and they want revenge.

There is absolutely no excuse for bullying someone. If you don't like a person, stay away from them – why make their lives hell?

If you suspect you may be bullying someone, it's you that needs help. You must:

- Stop bullying straight away. If your friends

carry it on because you were in a gang together tell them to stop too.
- Stop hanging out with friends who encourage bullying behaviour.
- Ask yourself why you were bullying. What drove you to do it? If it is personal, have it out one-on-one with the person you have the problem with. If they've upset you then make it clear how you feel – you won't achieve anything by going on about it, or by getting others involved.
- Learn to deal with your emotions in a more positive way. Bullying destroys the self-esteem of the bully, as well as the victim.
- Seek further help. There are lots of people willing to help you. It may even be that you are bullying because you are being bullied or abused yourself. You can make this stop. Parents, relatives, teachers or social workers will all be able to help you. But if you want to speak to a professional or somebody in complete confidence, then try contacting an organisation that specialises in bullying. (See helplines on pages 154–5.)

Whatever you do, make sure you don't carry on bullying. What would you do if the person you bullied killed themself? It may sound a bit dramatic, but it's happened before and it could easily happen again. You would have to live with the guilt for the rest of your life. So ask yourself again . . . is it worth it? We hope the answer is no.

APPENDIX

If you would like help or advice or even just to talk to someone, you could try contacting the following helplines:

Anti-bullying campaign
Offers counselling and advice
020 7378 1446

Careline
General crisis counselling – will help with any problem
020 8514 1177
Monday–Friday 10 a.m.–4 p.m. & 7p.m.–10 p.m.

Lesbian and Gay Switchboard
For info and advice
020 7837 7324
24/7

The Samaritans
General support
08457 909 090
24/7

Youth Access
Puts you in touch with services that can help
020 8772 9900
Monday–Friday 10 a.m.–1 p.m.

Youth 2 Youth
General advice from trained 14- to 23-year-olds
020 8896 3675
Monday & Thursday 6.30 p.m.–9.30 p.m.

INDEX

acquaintances 32
advice 6, 29, 48, 55–6
arguments 16–17, 112–13, 130, 131–3

being ignored 111–12
best friends 46–51, 115–19
betrayal 7, 13, 84–5, 100–9, 110–11
bitching (see under betrayal)
bossiness 36, 77–8, 93–4
boy magnets 35
boyfriends 119–21, 134–40
boys as friends 33–4, 134
bullying 147–53

companionship 6, 49
compromise 59
control freaks 36, 77–8

dependency 77, 82, 91, 98, 145 (see also under jealousy, and possessiveness)

fair-weather friends 31
fairness 53–60, 91–3
family 8–9, 17
feeling left out 80–2, 114–21, 142
forgiveness 16–17
fun 6, 14–15, 35, 37, 49, 75–6

hot–cold friends 31–2

inclusiveness 59, 80–2

keeping in touch 54–5, 59
kooky friends 35–6

leeches 37, 145
lending and helping 57–8
long-term friends 38
loneliness 10, 98, 144–5

maintaining friendships 58–60
making an effort 53–60, 90–1, 94–5
making friends 18–29, 143–4, 146
making mistakes 17, 78, 89–98

nastiness 82–3
new friendships 28–9 (see also under making friends)

party mates 37
popularity 95–6
problems 49–51, 79–88, 99–100
  bad influences 82–3, 87–8
  competitiveness 51, 123–4
  growing apart 85–7, 141–6
  jealousy 50, 51, 114–21, 122–6
  overkill 49–50
  possessiveness 50, 96–8

reassurance (see under understanding)
reliability (see under support)

school friends 19–21, 33
secrets (see under trust)
sense of humour 10, 14–15
sharing 46–7, 114–21
shyness 21, 25–7
support 7–8, 15–16, 49, 74–5, 76–7

trust 7–8, 13–14, 28, 29, 48, 77
trying too hard 90–93, 96

understanding 6, 8–10, 11–13, 34, 76–7

Also available from Piccadilly Press, by **MARIA COOLE**

BOYS – Just when you think you've got them sorted, they do something so bizarre you know you'll never get it right. But don't despair – Maria Coole is here to help! With humour, wit and the famous *Bliss* quizzes she'll help you understand:
- what boys really think;
- the pressures boys feel;
- what they like the most;
- what they worry about, and
- how to get one . . .

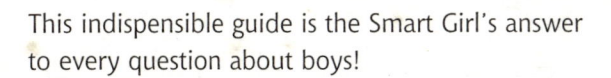

This indispensible guide is the Smart Girl's answer to every question about boys!

Also available in this series BLISS – THE SMART GIRL'S GUIDE TO SEX: *"This accessible and straightforward book . . . provides facts, reassurance and invaluable advice."* Starred Choice, Publishing News

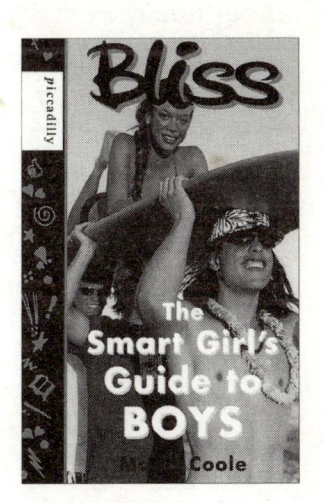

If you would like more information
about books available from Piccadilly Press
and how to order them, please
contact us at:

Piccadilly Press Ltd.
5 Castle Road
London
NW1 8PR

Tel: 020 7267 4492
Fax: 020 7267 4493

Feel free to visit our website at
www.piccadillypress.co.uk